HEALTH CARE COLLECTOR TRAINING GUIDE

Aspen Health & Administration Development Group

Gene Lass
Editor

Laura J. Merisalo
Contributing Editor

Sarah O. Rollman
Legal Editor

Introduction by
Ted M. Smith
Vice President of Programs
American Collectors Association
Minneapolis, Minnesota

AN ASPEN PUBLICATION®
Aspen Publishers, Inc.
Gaithersburg, Maryland
2000

Copyright © 2000 by Aspen Publishers, Inc.
A Wolters Kluwer Company
www.aspenpublishers.com
All rights reserved.

Jane Garwood, Publisher
Jo Gulledge, Executive Director
Kurt Lindblom, Acquisitions Editor
Steven Larose, Managing Editor
Gene Lass, Editor
Laura J. Merisalo, Contributing Editor
Marsha Davies, Editorial Coordinator
Rosette Graham, Senior Production Manager
Jennifer Fisher, Marketing Manager
Barbara Adams, Promotion Manager

Aspen Publishers, Inc. grants permission for photocopying for limited personal or internal use. This consent does not extend to other kinds of copying, such as copying for general distribution, for advertising or promotional purposes, for creating new collective works, or for resale. For more information, contact Aspen Publishers, Inc., Permissions Department, 200 Orchard Ridge Drive, Suite 200, Gaithersburg, MD 20878.

Orders: 800-638-8437
Customer Service: 800-234-1660

About Aspen Publishers • For more than 40 years, Aspen has been a leading professional publisher in a variety of disciplines. Aspen's vast information resources are available in both print and electronic formats. We are committed to providing the highest quality information available in the most appropriate format for our customers. Visit Aspen's Internet site for more information, resources, directories, articles, and a searchable version of Aspen's full catalog, including the most recent publications: **www.aspenpublishers.com**
   Aspen Publishers, Inc. • The hallmark of quality in publishing
      Member of the worldwide Wolters Kluwer group.

ISBN: 0-8342-1883-6

ISSN: 1530-7441

Printed in the United States of America

1 2 3 4 5

Table of Contents

Introduction v

Chapter 1 — Tips To Prioritize Accounts for Collection 1
    Prioritization: The Big Picture 2
    Organization: The Nitty-Gritty of Effective Collections 6
    Conclusion 10

Chapter 2 — Standard Collection Tips 13
    Organization and Cooperation Are Key 14
    Automated Assistance..................................... 15
    Effective Telephone Collection Techniques................. 16
    A Note on Timing 18
    First Impression Lasts 19
    General Collection Dos and Don'ts 20
    Overcoming Objections 21
    Motivating Patients To Pay............................... 24
    Identify Alternative Payment Sources 25
    Plan B... 26
    Securing a Promise To Pay 27
    Conclusion 28

Chapter 3 — Payer Tips.................................... 31
    Payer Review 32
    Patients Are a Nettlesome Payer Type 34
    It All Starts Up Front..................................... 35
    Being a Pest Is a Good Thing — With Caveats Included 37
    Human Relations Skills Are a Critical Collections Tool 37
    Clean Claims Come First 39
    Payer Collection Strategies 41
    Collection Strategies by Payer Type 44

Patients As Allies 49
Conclusion 51

Chapter 4 — Sample Collection Letters 53
How To Write a Collection Letter 54
Sample Collection Letters 57

Chapter 5 — Key Regulations 75
Truth in Lending Consumer Credit Cost Disclosure 75
Fair Credit Reporting Act 76
Fair Credit Billing Act 76
Fair Debt Collection Practices Act 77

Appendix A — Collector Resources 95
Professional Associations 96
Government Agencies via the Web 98
System Vendors and Outsourcing and Accounts Receivable
   Management Firms 99

Appendix B — Common Legal Questions 103

Appendix C — Starting an In-house Bank Loan Program 125
Full-Recourse Program Pays Off for Providers Even If
   Buyback Required 127
Identifying a Qualified Banking Partner 130
Revising Payment and Collections Policy 132
Employee Education and Training Are Critical for Success
   of Bank Financing Program 133
Bank Financing Basics 134
Credit Application Elements 136
The Patient Dialogue 140
Bank and Hospital Collection Policies In Sync 142
Conclusion 142

Introduction

Health care reimbursement is possibly one of the most complicated exchanges of money for service imaginable in today's world. After the various insurance companies have paid, there's often a balance still due — the patient's portion of the bill. Collection professionals charged with tracking down patient dollars that go past-due face a complicated maze of overlapping payers, managed care contracts, allowable charges, diagnostic codes, and general confusion by the public regarding who pays what, when, and why.

Whether they work for national hospital systems, small rural clinics, or third-party collection agencies, there is no denying that health care collectors play a vital role in today's health care economy. Every patient dollar recovered by a health care collector is a dollar the provider doesn't have to write off to bad debt. We're talking some serious dollars here. According to a December 1999 report released by the American Hospital Association, the hospital industry showed a gross revenue of $610 billion in 1998. With various industry studies estimating that bad debt is currently an average of 4.5 percent of hospitals' gross revenue, the approximate amount of revenue hospitals lost to bad debt in 1998 was $28 billion.

That's just the hospitals. Add debts written off by clinics, nursing homes, home health companies, and other types of providers, and the bad debt total becomes even more alarming. And let's face it, health care providers need every dollar owed to them just to survive in the face of falling reimbursements from government insurers, disputed and delayed payments from HMOs, and, of course, steadily rising costs for everything from tongue depressors to MRI technology.

There is also no arguing that health care collections is intellectually an extremely challenging profession. To effectively collect money from patients, a collector must understand the complexities of the insurance industry. Why? Quite simply, many patients don't understand their own insurance coverage and their level of personal responsibility for their health care bills. Many patients don't understand the services provided, how those services are billed, what portion of the bill the insurance is responsible for, what portion of the bill the patient is responsible for, what portion of the bill the insurance has already paid, or why the insurance denied payment. The health care collector has to have knowledge of health care billing and basic reimbursement policies for a wide variety of different payers to explain to the patients why they owe the balances being collected.

One of the roles of the health care collector is often simply to explain to the patient what is being charged, what has been paid, and why the balance is the responsibility of the patient. Often, bringing the patient to an understanding of the charges is enough to motivate the patient to pay. At other times, the collector faces a greater challenge in dealing with patients who are reacting emotionally rather than intellectually to the bill.

When the health care collector calls to ask for the money due, patients may be angry or depressed or simply apathetic about the bill. They are angry that the hospital stay costs so much. They are angry that the insurance denied the coverage. They are frightened because their illness is keeping them from working and the bills keep adding up. Or they are frightened because the money for the health care bill simply isn't in the budget. The challenge for health care collectors is to face emotional patients without becoming emotional themselves and to find an effective way of motivating patients to pay despite their anger or fear.

Training is essential to preparing health care collectors to take on the challenging role of financial advisor, psychologist, and motivational speaker. In addition to all the other knowledge and skills they must acquire, health care collectors should also be familiar with the Fair Debt Collection Practices Act, the Fair Credit Billing Act, the Fair Credit Reporting Act, and a variety of other federal and state legislation governing various aspects of the health care and collection industries.

As complicated as it is, the health care industry is also always changing. Continuing education and lifelong training should be the goal of every health care collection professional. The American Collectors Association and American Association of Healthcare Administrative Management recognize the hard work and commitment to lifelong learning that go into becoming a successful health care collection professional. Together, these two organizations have developed the Certified Healthcare Collection Specialist Exam — the only professional certification program recognized by both the health care and the collection industries. I would like to take this opportunity to invite you to consider the benefits that becoming a Certified Healthcare Collection Specialist can bring to your career.

Unfortunately, there is no quick and easy way to acquire the knowledge that makes a health care collector effective and efficient. Comprehensive knowledge of health care billing, payers, successful collection techniques, and various laws and regulations grows out of time, experience, and active study of the industry. The *Health Care Collector Training Guide* provides an excellent starting place, however. With information on face-to-face collections, telephone collections, collection letters, and other basic issues, this guide identifies the skills and information necessary to be successful in this complex industry.

So good luck to you, whether you are reading this training guide as an industry novice or as an experienced health care collector interested in refreshing your knowledge. Remember, despite the challenges noted above, and many more that we didn't have room for here, health care collections can also be very fulfilling. For individuals interested in working closely with a wide variety of people and in supporting the important role played by health care providers in our communities and lives, health care collections is not just another job — it is a satisfying career of which to be proud. Congratulations on choosing to be a health care collector!

— Ted M. Smith

Ted M. Smith is the vice president of programs for the American Collectors Association. He is also an advisor to several Aspen Publishers, Inc., publications, including the Hospital Accounts Receivable Analysis, the Receivables Report newsletter, and the Health Care Collector newsletter.

Chapter 1

Tips To Prioritize Accounts for Collection

Collecting in health care is becoming increasingly complex as managed care and its influences surface in all areas of accounts receivable management. Indeed, by the year 2005, managed care enrollment nationwide is expected to reach 111 million enrollees. National managed Medicare enrollment is expected to approach 11.5 million by 2005, and managed Medicaid is projected to reach 16.7 million enrollees.[1] Meanwhile, patients' financial obligations continue to mount due to rising copayment and deductible requirements. In addition, the dollars owed to health care provider organizations from commercial and government payers alike continue to constrict, making it critical that health care provider organizations collect quickly and efficiently the dollars due from myriad contracting payer organizations as well as from the patients they serve.

The question, then, becomes how best to tackle collection of these outstanding balances. The key is to prioritize accounts receivable to target accounts that offer the greatest potential return in the least amount of time. Collectors then must take that prioritization effort one step further in organizing the prioritized accounts within a work queue or work list to make the best use of time to effectively pursue collections and meet with success.

PRIORITIZATION: THE BIG PICTURE

There are several techniques to prioritize accounts. Top among them is to rank accounts receivable by dollar amounts, with high-dollar balances to receive immediate attention, be it a balance owed by a patient or an insurer.

A second and significant factor in prioritizing accounts is the date of service. Collection attempts should focus on claims that are closest to the date of service, whether these collection efforts are targeted to insurers or patients.

For insurers, collection efforts closest to the date of service are imperative because contractual requirements may frustrate collection efforts if the contract stipulates that claims must be received within a specific time frame after the date of service. Nonpayment of claims submitted within specified time constraints requires swift follow-up to determine the reason for denial and the necessary steps to reverse the denial and gain reimbursement.

For patients, the need for immediate collection efforts is imperative as it becomes increasingly difficult to collect from patients as time passes and patients no longer have a sense of urgency or acknowledge the link between health care services and payment. Indeed, collecting self-pay balances should be concentrated on the front end, prior to service or before discharge, when providers are most likely to meet with self-pay collection success as patients can more readily link service and payment issues. The following table shows how percent of collection success declines with time[2]:

Time of Collection Attempt	Percent of Collection Success
Before service	98%
At registration	85%
During service	70%
At discharge	61%
30 days after discharge	30%

However, if payment of self-pay balances is not garnered prior to discharge, collection of self-pay balances must be swift. As noted in the preceding table, success in collecting self-pay balances diminishes significantly after discharge, dropping to a mere 30 percent potential for success if collection attempts occur 30 days after discharge.

The reason self-pay collection success drops off so dramatically after discharge is rooted in patient payment priorities. Put another way, payment for health care services falls to the bottom of the payment priority list as patients weigh the consequences that may result from nonpayment of health care bills vs. nonpayment of other bills due. Health care services cannot be repossessed if patients don't pay. Therefore, patients who have received health care services and no longer are in need of treatment will be more inclined to disregard collection notices. Rather, other payment obligations — such as mortgage, car payments, rent, home or auto insurance, utilities, childcare, and the list goes on — take precedent as payment (or nonpayment) of these bills can place issues of daily living in jeopardy.

Health care collections is further complicated as health care delivery organizations struggle under reduced reimbursement, which often results in staff cutbacks. Staffing levels among health care providers have fluctuated quarterly over the past five years, at times showing staffing cuts, growth, or stability, reflecting the tumultuous times in the health care industry overall. Hospitals have reported average full-time equivalent (FTE) staffing levels devoted to accounts receivable management as low as 30.2 FTEs in 1995, with a high of 45.9 FTEs in early 1999.[3]

This staffing data highlights the need to establish and secure a proactive approach to collecting outstanding accounts receivable. A proactive collection strategy is imperative to make the most effective use of human resources and allow employees to be most productive and to succeed in their collection efforts.

Prioritization Techniques To Create Collection Work Lists

A proactive approach to collections calls for an ability to prioritize accounts that will be worked by employees, as well as an ability to recognize which accounts will not be handled by staff and rather will be routed through an automated collections follow-up procedure or immediately outsourced to an outside agency.

To prioritize collection accounts, take the following three steps:
1. **Identify high-dollar balances.**

    Logic dictates that collection of high-dollar accounts receive swift and immediate attention. It is the 80-20 rule at work, with 80 percent of the revenue generated from fewer than 20 percent of the accounts. Absent a process to rank accounts by any other method, the high-dollar balance prioritization is the most common method relied upon in tackling health care collections.

    High-dollar balances should receive top priority, regardless of financial class or any other account profiling that may occur. For example, a high-dollar account that is self-pay may appear to be a lost cause based on demographic and other patient data on hand. However, by placing a call to the patient, collections employees learn whether collection on the account is indeed possible, be it through securing a bank loan for the patient or perhaps retrospectively enrolling the patient in a government program, such as Title IX.

    High-dollar accounts should be ranked by balance increments, working the very highest balances first and moving down.

2. **Establish a small-balance limit.**

    As high-dollar balances rise to the top of the collections priority list, a natural byproduct is the small-balance limit, or the amount under which there is inadequate staffing to manually work these low-dollar accounts.

    Identifying the small-balance limit can be done by tracking just how far down the collections priority list employees get in working accounts. If employees are consumed by working accounts with balances of $1,500 or more and never get below that account balance, for example, then the small-balance limit may be $1,500.

    This minimum balance, then, is the amount below which accounts are handled through an automated process rather than through spending human resources to chase after these low-dollar balances. Depending on the size of the facility, the small-balance limit may be under $250 or up to $1,000 or more. For accounts that fit into this category, collections should be automated so that the accounts remain active without the need for manual intervention.

For example, if an account is at or below a $500 small-balance limit, a tracer is sent automatically if payment isn't received within specified time parameters. If it is an insurance claim, the system may be set up so that it automatically converts the balance to self-pay if the insurer fails to pay within a specified time frame.

Failing receipt of payment from the patient, the system will automatically refer the account to the collections agency contracted with the provider to handle delinquent accounts.

If small-balance accounts cannot be routed through an automated tracking and follow-up system, a provider organization should consider dedicating an employee to handle low-dollar account balances or to outsource these accounts immediately, while they are fresh and most likely to generate revenue.

3. **Segregate accounts by financial class.**

With a small-balance limit established and accounts that remain in need of manual intervention by collections employees being the high-dollar claims, these high-dollar accounts can be further ranked by financial class. Health care organizations often want to prioritize accounts this way, as working a Medicare claim is different than working a claim with a commercial payer. Collection approaches for different commercial payers also will vary. Plus, collection techniques effective with government or commercial payers are different than those used to successfully collect from patients with self-pay balances.

The size of the organization and the number of contracts held will determine how to segregate financial classes. For smaller institutions, collections employees may specialize in managed care more generically, while a larger institution may dedicate collections employees to handle accounts with a specific payer. At larger facilities, further splits within a payer also may be warranted if a payer's enrollees comprise a large portion of the patient mix. In such cases, several FTEs may be devoted to a specific payer, with each handling accounts determined and assigned by an alpha-split.

Although prioritizing accounts by financial class can be set aside in deference to prioritizing based on high-dollar balances alone, incorporating financial class into the process is popular and effective as specialized collection techniques for each payer increasingly are required to maximize collection success.

A Word on Date-of-Service Prioritization

While the goal of any health care provider organization is to bill in a timely manner so that reimbursement is obtained with minimal collections follow-up required, there always will be exceptions. For example, while it is often asserted that managed care accounts should be 30-day receivables, health care collectors will attest that all too often, that is not the case, as their workloads will prove.

The goal should be to give attention to accounts early on and to identify slow payers so that, in addition to collections follow-up, there is executive follow-up by members of the provider's health care contracting team. Health plans that are required by contract to pay within 30 days but routinely fail to uphold that obligation must be brought to the attention of negotiators on the provider's contracting team.

Date of service becomes more of a critical issue in clean-up efforts, when aging accounts need to be resolved with aggressive collection efforts that either bring in the money or definitively determine accounts that should be written off as charity or bad debt.

ORGANIZATION: THE NITTY-GRITTY OF EFFECTIVE COLLECTIONS

Given a prioritized work list, collectors must fit that into a well-defined and organized collection strategy. Effective collections follow-up hinges on organization. Collectors must not only organize and prioritize accounts assigned to them, but also organize their daily routine to ensure that the best efforts are put forth at the proper time to be most effective in securing reimbursement.

The daily routine for a collector can be broken down into time segments and tasks that must be accomplished within those times. Also, it is important that collectors make efficient use of time. The most productive collectors don't have down time. Rather, time on hold is time for filing, organizing, or preparing for the next call.

Create an Effective Workspace and System

Organizing your workspace and files is a key first step. Here are several ways to do that:

- Develop a manual or electronic collection note card system that allows you to document account activity and note dates for further follow up.
- Develop a tickler system so that you are able to stay on top of your accounts.

  If using an electronic system, the system will do much of the work for you in terms of sorting accounts and pulling up prioritized accounts on the date that follow-up action is required. Systems vary in sophistication, and many collectors don't have the benefit of an automated system. However, a manual tickler file can be just as effective. It can be as simple as a system that uses files labeled with each day of the month. As you make calls that require further follow-up, note the date that action is required and place the account in the corresponding file. When that day arrives, the file is complete with account information and required follow-up for that day.

- Develop a system to track calls placed.

  Making a printout of a collections work list can aid in quickly identifying the status of follow-up efforts. For instance, accounts for which calls have been made can be highlighted and noted with the time the calls were placed. You then know which accounts are awaiting a return call. You are also able to track the length of time since a message was placed and try again at a later time or at a different time the following day if no return call is received.

- Highlight accounts with a color reserved only for accounts that require daily follow-up until resolved.

Prioritize Work List

Prioritizing accounts within a work queue requires the same techniques used in creating the work queue, but on a smaller scale. To prioritize accounts within your work list, do the following:

- Group accounts by payer.

    Work lists contain prioritized accounts by dollar balance and/or age. However, it is inefficient to call payers about a single high-dollar account when there are several other claims outstanding. Rather, pull together all accounts for a single payer so that in one call, you can inquire about the payment status for multiple accounts. Your first query will be on the high-dollar claim, but you should be prepared to follow up with queries on at least four or five other accounts, if not more.

- Identify payers with poor payment history.

    These are the payers who put you on hold forever, never return calls, or rarely are able to provide payment status for claims upon the first request. These payers should be called first so that you establish the initial contact and can follow up the same day if the payer is unable to provide you with a suitable response.

Use Call Time Effectively

Once your workspace is organized and accounts are prioritized by payer, ensure that you are able to make the most effective use of your call time. You should be placing calls to payers first thing in the morning, the best time to reach insurer representatives.

To make the best use of your call time, follow these suggestions:

- Keep calls to five or 10 minutes, excluding hold time.

    Setting time parameters for a call will help you to remain focused and stick to the point.

- Use hold time effectively.

    When insurers place you on hold, use that time to begin planning your next call, to examine your work list to identify other accounts to be grouped by insurer, or to do other paperwork.

- Plan calls.

This step ties in with prioritization of accounts on your work list. When making a call, ensure that you are making an inquiry for all outstanding claims to avoid making repeated calls — and exposing yourself to repeated hold time — with the same payer.

Daily Workflow

Although actual collections is anything but routine, the daily workflow should follow a fairly set routine. This routine is determined by how to get the most out of your collection efforts. As noted, mornings should be dedicated to contacting payers to obtain claim status and speed payment. The outcomes of these calls will determine the specific tasks for the afternoon.

For self-pay collections, collectors should set aside one evening a week to place calls to patients. This time should be dedicated to making the calls, as the window of time to contact patients is limited. Additional follow-up required, such as resending a "lost" bill, can then be done in the afternoon of the following day.

In general, collectors can optimize their collection efforts by devoting afternoon hours to do the following:

- Follow through with payer information requests to enable payment.

    Again, organize your work. Sort claims by the type of follow-up information required. For example, if several payers request further information from medical records, gather the claims that require this additional information so that you are gathering data for multiple accounts at the same time, rather than continuously running to medical records. Or, if explanations of benefits (EOBs) are required, go to the file cabinet to seek EOBs for multiple accounts rather than jumping up and going to the file cabinet each time the need for an EOB arises.
- Follow through with rebills for payers (and patients) who state no record of the claim.
- For payers that accept fax requests for claims status, create a batch of claims and submit fax requests, making a note to follow up in

the morning to verify receipt of the fax and obtain status of those claims.
- Organize accounts for the next day.

    Review your tickler file. Sort and group by payer new or existing accounts for follow-up the next day. The goal is to create a system so that when you arrive, you can begin dialing, not begin figuring out whom to call on what accounts.

Special note: When setting follow-up dates for claims, use the same date for accounts with the same payer. That way, multiple accounts for the same payer are worked at the same time, rather than piecemeal with repeated contacts to the payer. Use the earliest date for follow-up for the accounts.

This does not mean that a $50,000 account with high priority should not be singled out for daily or 48-hour follow-up. However, it is more efficient to get as many accounts before a payer as possible rather than one at a time. The high-dollar claim might be worked daily, with inquiries on all other claims occurring again within five days.

Another option is to contact certain payers on certain days. You might contact ABC Health Plan on Mondays, XYZ Health Plan on Tuesdays, and so forth. Depending on the size of your facility and the number of patients covered, a single health plan a day might be a full plate. In some cases, working two or three payers a day might be more appropriate.

CONCLUSION

Successful health care collections is a blend of science and art, with a heavy emphasis on common sense and logic. It is important to identify core competencies within the organization and maximize the potential collections result by focusing on these core competencies.

If collectors routinely fail to get to accounts below $500, automate the collections process for these accounts. Or, barring the ability to automate collections follow-up on low-dollar accounts, consider sending those accounts to an agency that specializes in such collections and can dedicate the time and effort needed to turn those accounts into positive cash flow. It may cost a little, but paying a percentage of the amount collected to an outside agency is preferable to writing off an account to bad debt because it languished untouched in your system for too long to obtain any payment.

If an outside agency can do it better and/or cheaper, outsourcing may be the best alternative so that internal collections employees can implement a proactive strategy rather than constantly scrambling to catch up as accounts continue to age.

Prioritizing accounts allows providers to stay on top of the collections game, particularly as employees are dedicated to specific payer groups so that specialized collection techniques can be implemented to allow for effective and successful collections from all payer types, be they patients, commercial carriers, or government health plans.

REFERENCES

1. *InterStudy HMO Forecasting Report* (Minneapolis: InterStudy Publications, January 2000).
2. *The Health Care Registration and Admitting Manual* (Gaithersburg, MD: Aspen Publishers, Inc., 1994).
3. *HARA (Hospital Accounts Receivable Analysis)*, quarterly reports from 1995 through 1999 (Gaithersburg, MD: Aspen Publishers, Inc.).

SOURCES CONSULTED

Lori Zindl, president, Outsource Inc., Pewaukee, Wisconsin.
Steve Carroll, president, Medical Recovery System Inc., Cincinnati, Ohio.

CHAPTER 2

Standard Collection Tips

Although collecting in health care has evolved and continues to evolve with the health care industry, at a certain level, very little has changed. As has always been the case, health care collectors must diligently and assertively pursue reimbursement from all payers, including patients, the government, and other third-party payers.

A collector's approach must always be professional, courteous, and timely. It's difficult to communicate a sense of urgency for any debtor to pay an outstanding balance if the facility has failed to initiate contact and follow-up in a timely manner. In turn, patients are less likely to respond to a collector who communicates in a brusque, unprofessional manner.

A vast majority of hospital executives, nearly 77 percent, believe their facilities have an effective collections policy. However, only 29 percent of these executives reported that collection calls to patients were made within 30 days of discharge, with more than a third reporting that collection calls were placed to patients within 90 days. Another 12 percent reported that patients never receive a call from collections staff about balance due amounts.[1]

Clearly, there is room for improvement.

A key first step in collecting is to prioritize accounts, as discussed in Chapter 1. Then, the collector's work begins in earnest. It requires effective organization skills, good timing, an assertive and professional manner, and effective tracking of collections activity so that the necessary follow-up and follow-through occurs in a timely manner.

The need to pursue collections in a timely manner is imperative, as the window of opportunity for successful collections is limited. For example:

Account age	0-30 days	31-60 days	61-90 days	91-120 days	181-210 days	271-300 days	1 year	2 years
Collectability	98%	95%	84%	78%	58%	40%	22%	10%

The best opportunity to collect from any payer type is within the first 30 days. Three months out, the likelihood that accounts will be collected falls to slightly more than 70 percent. Attempts to collect on accounts more than six months old will present a mere 50-50 chance for collection.

It is incumbent upon collectors, therefore, to move swiftly to take advantage of the patient's increased inclination to pay when services and payment are within close proximity. If patient-pay balances are not collected at the time of service, collection follow-up within 30 days is crucial.

ORGANIZATION AND COOPERATION ARE KEY

Once accounts are prioritized, collectors must develop effective systems to organize and track accounts and related collection activity. Take the time to gather detailed information before initiating contact with a payer. Before initiating a call, basic information that must be at your fingertips includes:
- responsible party
- past payment record
- past collection activity
- the outstanding balance and how long it is overdue

This information should be available from your facility's file on the patient, beginning with the information taken at registration and continuing through records of care given and payment options taken. Without accurate, timely information, a patient's record is virtually useless and the difficulty in collecting the account increases geometrically. Therefore, all departments must cooperate in updating and sharing all information in the patient's file.

Knowing the details of accounts is imperative so that any questions that may be raised by a payer or patient can be answered promptly during the collections call, and objections to payment can be overcome. For instance, if a patient indicates she was unaware of an outstanding balance and states she never received a bill, the collector needs to be able to respond with the date the bill was mailed, the amount due, and the due date for the payment.

If collectors fail to provide detailed account information, the patient is left with the impression that the collector is disorganized and doesn't have a handle on the account. This erodes credibility in the eyes of patients and leaves them with an impression that payment is not a priority for the facility.

Detailed documentation of account activity also builds credibility in the eyes of patients. This is where effective tracking comes into play. If calls have been placed, messages left, or patients have returned calls, an effective collector will have that information documented. For instance, if a patient states that he understood his insurance carrier would be billed for the services, a collector must be able to quickly identify and respond with third-party collections activity for that account. For example, the collector needs to assure the patient that the insurer has been billed for the portion of services covered by his carrier, and that an outstanding balance remains the patient's responsibility, which is the purpose for the call.

AUTOMATED ASSISTANCE

Automated collection follow-up systems that organize and prioritize calls increasingly are the norm for many provider collection offices. Such a system allows all information on collection activity to be documented in one place, showing the date and outcome of a collection attempt and the next contact date for follow-up.

Lacking an automated follow-up system, collectors can effectively manage collection activity with collection note cards that are filed by the day of the month. This is commonly called a "tickler file." Collection activity is documented on the collection record for the account, which is then filed in the folder marked with the corresponding date set for follow-up. Each day, the file for that date is pulled, and within it are accounts in need of follow-up and related records and documentation.

EFFECTIVE TELEPHONE COLLECTION TECHNIQUES

With detailed documentation of an account in hand, a telephone call can be placed. Collectors will achieve greater success in telephone collections if they follow these eight steps in establishing contact and securing a commitment to pay:

1. **Identify the patient or responsible party.**

    This simple step requires the collector to ensure that the person on the other end of the line is the person responsible for payment. Ask for the patient by his or her full name — Mr. Richard Jones rather than simply Mr. Jones — to avoid mistakenly speaking to the wrong person.

    Once the responsible party is on the line, continue to refer to the person as Mr., Mrs., or Ms., as a sign of respect and a mark of professionalism.

2. **Identify yourself and your organization.**

    This step comes after identifying the responsible party for a key reason: If the patient doesn't want to speak with you, knowing immediately that it's Ms. (your name) from (your facility) allows the patient to screen and decline the call.

    If asked to identify yourself, you must. Identify yourself as Mr. or Ms. (your name) with (your organization or facility), so as to further convey professionalism and set a business tone for the relationship. According to federal law, collectors must reveal their intent and identity when contacting patients. Furthermore, some state laws make it illegal for collectors to use on-the-job aliases when collecting.

3. **Ask for payment in full.**
    Once you have patients on the telephone, don't beat around the bush. Tell them you are calling about their outstanding balance of (amount) for services received on (date of care), which was due (date due) and is now overdue. Then ask when payment in full will be made or if they would prefer to put the outstanding balance on a credit card.
4. **Pause.**
    Silence is golden, and a well-timed pause is critical so that patients can respond with when they will pay or why they can't pay. This pause allows them to take ownership and responsibility for the payment request.
5. **Listen.**
    Patients will typically respond in one of two ways. First, they may be apologetic, stating they overlooked the bill and will take care of it immediately. Frequently, however, they will offer some type of excuse, such as they never received the bill, they don't understand the bill, they thought insurance would cover the services, they think the bill is inaccurate, or some other excuse.
    It's important to listen to patients and allow them to tell their story so that you can effectively respond.
6. **Respond by overcoming the objection.**
    This is perhaps the most critical element of a collections call. It requires listening intently to the objection to payment so that you can properly respond and overcome the objection.
    For example, if a patient states a belief that the bill is inaccurate, you can then state that you have the bill before you and ask what portion of the bill is in question. This readiness and ability to target the issue on the spot and respond is imperative. Patients will then realize that you are up to speed on the status of the account and the billed charges and can tackle any issues related to the account.
7. **Secure a commitment.**
    Assuming that you have effectively overcome patients' objections to pay, now is the time to gain a commitment from them to

send in payment. If patients' questions were answered and the bill is no longer in question, you can confidently ask for payment in full and ask the patient for a date when payment can be expected. If outstanding questions remain, then gain a commitment on when this issue will be resolved. For example, if patients state they want to contact their insurer about an amount they feel should be covered, set a date for when you will follow up to learn the outcome of the call.

8. **Confirm arrangements.**

   This step is important as it conveys to patients that the call will result in some action. For instance, if patients state they need to wait for their next paycheck, confirmation would be that you will expect payment on (date discussed), after they get paid, and you will contact them if payment is not received by that date. If patients state they want to pursue a coverage issue with their insurer, determine a date by which the patient will make that contact as well as a date when you will follow up to learn the outcome of the patient's inquiry with their insurer.

   In confirming arrangements with patients, it's effective to have them restate the agreement you have reached together to secure payment. By doing so, patients are forced to take ownership and responsibility for their role in ensuring the account is paid. For example, say to the patient, "I'm happy we've come to an agreement. Are you sure you understand the details?"

A NOTE ON TIMING

When contacting patients, timing is critical — including the time of day, the time of week, and the time of month. The best time to reach patients is in the evening hours, when they are home from work and back from picking up the children from after-school activities. Collectors should schedule at least one day a week when they work into the evening hours to contact patients. The best days are Monday through Thursday, when patients are in the mindset of taking care of daily living chores and responsibilities rather than planning for down time on the weekend.

The best time of the month is in the middle, from the 15th to about the 25th. *The reason:* Most people get paid at two-week intervals, and most bills are due early in the month. By calling patients mid-month, collectors are more likely to connect with patients when they have just been paid but have not yet committed those dollars to first-of-the-month bills.

FIRST IMPRESSION LASTS

In initiating contact with patients, it's important that you make a good first impression and remain businesslike and professional. While it's important to establish a friendly, respectful, and courteous rapport with patients, don't overdo it. Patients know the reason for the call and won't appreciate what they will perceive as insincere inquiries, such as, "How are you?" This simple query may sound harmless enough, but it could open the floodgates to your hearing complaints about their health despite recent services, which will hurt your chances of collection. Or, patients will sense that you are trying to butter them up before getting to the point.

Think about how you feel when a telephone solicitor says, "Hello, may I speak with Mr. Jones? Oh, hello, Mr. Jones, how are you today?" You know they don't really care about how you are doing and have only one goal — to sell you on something that you likely don't want.

Patients who owe you money will have a similar response. Although they may feign otherwise, they typically know the reason for the call, and will appreciate a more direct approach rather than disingenuous attempts to win them over.

In establishing a rapport with patients over the telephone, it is important to remain professional and stick to the point without being overbearing or coming across as a bully. Statements like, "We must receive payment ..." will not win you cooperation from patients. Rather, such tactics will open the door to complaints about poor customer service and calls to a supervisor, which will result in indefinite delays in payment.

If details of an account are disputed, do not argue with patients. Identify the item in question, and then provide patients with evidence that the bill is indeed correct. In doing so, you extend patients respect and allow them to maintain their dignity in contesting a charge. You need to allow patients the ability to question the bill, and then be able to provide assurance and proof that the bill is correct.

If you are unable to justify the disputed charge, let patients know you will look into it immediately, and then ask for payment in full on the balance minus the disputed charge.

Or, if the bill is indeed incorrect, take action to rectify the error. Then return promptly to the issue of payment. Collection efforts are now enhanced, particularly if the error was in the patient's favor, as the patient sees that you are responsive and competent in handling his or her concerns.

GENERAL COLLECTION DOS AND DON'TS

As stated earlier, it's important to quickly and firmly establish patients' responsibility to pay, and then allow them to take ownership of that responsibility and meet their financial obligations. To aid you in that endeavor, be certain to do the following:
- Know details about the account.
- Remain calm and cheerful.
- Remain committed to seeking payment in full.
- Treat patients as you would want to be treated.
- Remember the customer is always right.
- Perform timely follow-up when details of the account are disputed.

On the other hand, to establish and maintain a positive and professional rapport, there are certain things you should not do when contacting patients:
- Avoid antagonizing patients.
- Never raise your voice to patients.
- Never accuse patients of being irresponsible or dishonest for failing to pay their bill.
- Never threaten patients.
- Don't dig in your heels and take on a hard-nosed attitude.

OVERCOMING OBJECTIONS

A critical step in effective collection strategies is overcoming patient objections to payment. Objections are many and varied, from "never got a bill," to "my spouse handles that."

Regardless of the objection, collectors must have a response, and this response must be carefully thought out. The response must be carefully worded and expressed with the right tone. Remember, never argue with patients. While you may win an argument, you may lose payment in full, and you certainly hurt patient relations and satisfaction.

In overcoming patients' objections to payment:

- *Use intelligence, not emotion.* Patients may become emotional. You need to remain empathic and businesslike.
- *Use a professional and businesslike manner.* Be friendly, but not too familiar. Stick to business-related matters.
- *Be courteous.* Always consider the other person's feelings. Be polite.
- *Be flexible.* Your collection approach may need to be changed based on what you learn from patients. And you need to be able to adapt your style and approach to better match the patient. People respond better when other people speak at the same rate as them and in similar tones. If the patient speaks quietly or slowly, you should do the same. If the patient speaks very informally, try to be more friendly while still being professional.
- *Be natural.* Inasmuch as you are making an important business call about an outstanding balance due, try to be conversational. Avoid technical jargon. Opt instead for simple, uncomplicated words or phrases to engage patients in a payment discussion that will lead to a resolution that is acceptable to both.

With this foundation, the ability to overcome objections to payment is eased. Statements from patients like, "I have more important bills to pay," or, "I'm unemployed and can't pay," can be tackled with professional ease and finesse if you adhere to the basic tenets of effective collections noted above. Overcoming objections is something that must be handled effectively and swiftly because the sooner you overcome the objection, the closer you are to receiving payment.

Some common examples of objections and sample responses are as follows:

Excuse	Response
"I never had to pay at time of service before."	*"I understand your concern, but changes in office procedure were needed to contend with the rising costs of health care. Paying at the time of service helps us avoid additional administrative costs, which saves you money. Plus, it lets you take care of your payment now rather than worry about a bill later. Would you like to pay by cash, check, or credit card?"*
"My insurance will pay."	*"We verified your insurance coverage, and the representative noted a deductible/copayment obligation that is your responsibility. Would you like to pay by cash, check, or credit card?"*
"I didn't bring my checkbook."	*"That's okay. We accept cash and credit cards as well."*
"Can I pay over time?"	The response here will vary, depending on the facility's payment policies. Those policies may include anything from bank loans to partial payments made within a specific period of time. Example: *"You can pay half now and the remaining half in 30 days. Or, if you pay in full now, you will be entitled to a 5 percent discount. How would you like to handle your payment?"* Tip: Don't let payment plans stretch out over long periods of time. Partial payments should be structured so

continues

Excuse	Response
	payment in full is obtained within three months or less. Again, payment plans will vary depending on facility policies and/or individual circumstances of patients. Be flexible, but don't give away the store.
"I saw the doctor for only five minutes. Why is the bill so high?"	"The office visit cost is based on the quality of care and counsel, not the time with the physician. Our physicians are among the best in the area, which is often reflected in our pricing structure. And our costs are competitive with those of other facilities."
"My doctor told me not to worry about a bill."	"Your physician didn't mean you wouldn't have to pay, but that you shouldn't worry about the bill because our payment policies allow us some flexibility. We arrange payment schedules to match your circumstances." Follow this up with the response listed for "Can I pay over time?"
"I can't afford to pay, and the doctor knew that. I don't understand why the doctor sent me in for tests knowing I couldn't pay."	"The tests were a necessary part of the treatment. If they had been elective procedures, we could have waited to schedule the tests when you were in a better financial position. However, since the tests were required immediately, let's figure out a payment plan to meet your needs and our requirements." Again, follow this up with the response to "Can I pay over time?"

continues

Excuse	Response
"You seem more worried about the bill than my care."	"I assure you we are concerned about your care first. And payment for that care ensures that we can continue to provide the quality treatment you and other patients expect."
"Just send me a bill."	"I'm sorry, we can no longer delay collecting payments."

MOTIVATING PATIENTS TO PAY

Once payment objections are tackled, you are in a position to tap into patient motivations to pay. There are three primary factors that motivate people to pay: pride, honesty, and fear. People take pride in paying bills on time, achieving a good credit record, and avoiding additional costs that may be incurred through interest charges or late fees. In addition, most people have a sense of fair play, and they know that making good on their financial obligations is the right and fair thing to do. Lastly, people don't want their failure to make good on a debt to land them in the hands of a collection agency or cause them to face legal action.

The collector's job, then, is to tap into those motivations to successfully collect an account. Effective collection techniques will reveal to patients the benefits of paying their health care bills.

While it sounds cliché, attitude is everything. It is important for collectors to be positive and professional in conveying the need for patients to pay. Don't paint the prospect of paying a health care bill with a black brush. Share with patients the benefits of taking care of their financial obligations to your facility to motivate them to pay. The benefits and the phrases that help convey those benefits to patients are as follows:

Benefit	Message to Patient
Maintain or establish a good credit record	*"A good credit record with our institution will help assure that you will have access to credit when you need it for other purchases, loans or other borrowing."* Make it clear to patients that, as with any other debt, failure to pay their health care bills in full can affect their credit if you're forced to send their account to a collection agency.
Peace of mind in knowing financial obligations have been met	*"By taking care of this bill today, you won't have to worry about it any more."*
Avoid future collection activity	*"By paying in full now, you can avoid future collection activity."*
Avoid additional expense	*"By paying in full now, you can avoid possible additional expense later."*
Sense of fairness	*"We appreciate your reliance upon us to provide you with our best service. This level of service is possible because patients like you follow through on your financial obligations."*

IDENTIFY ALTERNATIVE PAYMENT SOURCES

Knowing that most patients want to pay, the greatest obstacle to collecting on an account is that the patient doesn't have the cash on hand. Collectors can work with patients to uncover financial resources that are not obvious. Patients may believe they are unable to pay because the amount due isn't currently available in their checking account and they are at their credit card limit. However, there are alternative payment sources that a collector can suggest. Among them are the following:

Loan Sources	Cash Sources	Money for Monthly Payment
employer	tax refund	payroll check
insurance policy	stocks, bonds	second job
bank or credit union	savings bonds	income from hobby
relatives or friends	savings accounts	spouse's payroll check
finance company		unemployment check
payroll advance		military reserve pay
mortgage		pension
consolidated loans		sick pay
		bonus pay

Source: *The Health Care Registration and Admitting Manual,* Aspen Publishers, Inc., © 1994.

Identifying alternative payment sources has another key benefit: It provides patients with options and allows them to choose how to make payment. Patients are more willing and apt to pay if they are making the choice to do so and how, rather than being forced to do so.

PLAN B

Although payment in full should always be the goal, collectors need to have a back-up plan. The back-up plan may be to refer the patient to a bank loan program, or to agree to partial payments over a short period of time.

Although discounting should be avoided if possible, it can be an effective tool to motivate patients to pay, as many patients will seize the opportunity for a "good deal." For example, a patient who owes a facility $500 and states that he can pay only $25 a month will leave the provider with an outstanding balance on the account for nearly two years. Worse, the provider will incur ongoing collection costs to track payment and follow up as needed during that two-year period. With an average cost to collect ranging from $0.023 to $0.053 per dollar collected,[2] it may be in the provider's best financial interest to offer a 5 percent discount to avoid future collection costs and lost interest income.

A word of caution: Word of discounts spreads quickly in a payer community, among patients or third-party payers, which can hamper collection efforts. Patients aware that discounts are offered to clear up outstanding balances may opt to hold back payment until the facility is willing to extend a discount to get them to pay up. Discounts are more common on the front end — for example, securing payment at the time of service by offering a prompt-pay discount — which is seen as a more appropriate reward. Extending discounts further down the line creates the perception that patients are rewarded for slow payment.

SECURING A PROMISE TO PAY

Once payment objections are overcome and patients are motivated to pay, securing a promise to pay is possible. Be alert to signs that the patient is ready and willing to pay. Such signs include questions from the patients such as, "How much is the bill?" or "How much time do I have to pay?" or "Can I make monthly payments?"

When it becomes apparent that patients are prepared to make payment arrangements, it is time to secure a promise to pay. Effectively securing a promise to pay requires that the payment promise is clearly articulated and agreed upon by the patient. Seven steps to secure a promise to pay include the following:

1. **Be specific.**

    Get a commitment for the exact payment amount and date of payment. Don't let patients go with the statement, "I will mail payment this week." Rather, set a date for when payment can be expected, and let patients know you are noting that in your records and will follow up with them if it is not received.

2. **Be realistic.**

    Make sure that the amount the patient promises to pay by a certain date is possible. If the payment arrangements are unrealistic, the patient is unlikely to follow through with any payment at

all. It is better to secure realistic payment arrangements, rather than set the patient up for failure in paying on the account.
3. **Review the rules.**

    Let patients know your expectations based on the promise to pay. For example, if the patient promises to pay a $300 debt in three installments, attach due dates for each payment and let the patient know you will follow up to seek payment in full if the payments are not made.
4. **Create urgency.**

    Repeat the payment terms two or three times to create a sense of urgency in keeping payments current.
5. **Follow up on time.**

    If payment is not received by the date agreed upon, follow up in a timely fashion. Follow-up collection calls should be made within 24 to 48 hours after a missed payment. The sense of urgency is lost if you forget to call when a payment is overdue.
6. **Follow through.**

    If your payment agreement with patients is that payment in full is required if a payment is missed, follow through in seeking payment in full. If not, you will lose credibility with patients.
7. **Avoid extending a third chance.**

    If patients break the first promise to pay, you may extend a second chance, but not a third. By this time, it is apparent that the patient will not follow through on promises to pay. The account then becomes a candidate for a collection agency.

CONCLUSION

Although a great deal of ground must be covered in making collection calls, it is territory that should be covered in a limited time frame. Collection calls should be limited to five or 10 minutes in length. Lengthier calls indicate an inability to stay focused and zero in on the reason for the call.

Effective collections require good organizational skills in preparing for a call, effective tracking and documentation of collection activity, and timely follow-up. These strategies must be buttressed with personable but professional communication skills, which are critical to engage patients in a conversation that they would prefer to avoid. No one likes talking about money, especially if it concerns an outstanding debt patients are either unwilling to pay or believe they are unable to pay.

A good collector is persuasive, has good timing, is skilled in the art of negotiation, and accomplishes goals with a positive attitude.

Working in your favor is that most people want to pay their bills and make good on their promises to pay. Key, then, is to effectively negotiate payment arrangements that extend patients dignity and respect while gaining a commitment to pay that is realistic. This creates a win-win situation, with the facility gaining reimbursement and patients being able to take pride in knowing they have fulfilled their payment obligations in a timely manner and in a way that fits within their budget.

REFERENCES

1. *HARA (Hospital Accounts Receivable Analysis)*, second quarter 1999 (Gaithersburg, MD: Aspen Publishers, Inc.).
2. *HARA (Hospital Accounts Receivable Analysis)*, fourth quarter 1999 (Gaithersburg, MD: Aspen Publishers, Inc.).

SUGGESTED READING

Health Care Collector, Vol. 12, No. 6 (Gaithersburg, MD: Aspen Publishers, Inc., 1999).

Chapter 3

Payer Tips

As with any collection effort, timeliness is a top priority when seeking reimbursement from commercial and government payers. Ideally, health care provider organizations should have systems and processes in place to ensure that payers that fail to respond to a submitted claim within 20 days — be it with a payment, denial, information request, or other response — receive a follow-up call and request for payment.

Such a call serves as a reminder and prod for payers to submit reimbursement within time frames specified in the contract. Or, if there is a problem with the claim, the resolution effort can begin in earnest, prior to the account aging significantly and becoming more difficult to collect.

Timely follow-up is particularly important with large-dollar accounts. Contact should be made with payers within a week or two of submitting a claim on large-dollar accounts, to ensure receipt of the claim and to set the stage for timely reimbursement.

Keep in mind, effective collections requires shaping perceptions and creating a sense of urgency. Allowing claims to age beyond 30 days or, worse, up to 90 days or more before diligent follow-up attempts occur creates the perception among payers that the claim is not a high priority.

PAYER REVIEW

Hospitals' major payers fall into two broad categories: government and commercial health plans. Government health plans include Medicare, Medicaid (Title XIX), and CHAMPUS or TRICARE. Commercial plans include traditional indemnity and managed care health plans and various hybrids that may be local, regional, or national health plans with a variety of plan offerings.

Medicare

This is a federal entitlement program that provides health care benefits to individuals over 65 years of age, the blind, the disabled, and individuals with kidney failure. In general, Medicare Part A covers inpatient and outpatient hospital visits, and Medicare Part B covers physician visits, pharmacy, and other health care services.

Medicare beneficiaries also have the option to enroll in managed Medicare plans, or Medicare+Choice. The most current data show that slightly more than 20 percent of all Medicare beneficiaries are enrolled in a managed Medicare plan.

Special Notes

Documenting medical necessity is a must under the Medicare program. Lacking proof of medical necessity, Medicare likely will deny the claim. If medical necessity is in question, providers must secure an advance beneficiary notice (ABN) prior to service that allows the provider to bill patients for claims that are denied due to lack of medical necessity. If the ABN is not secured prior to service, there is no collection recourse and the denied claim must be written off as a loss.

It is imperative when processing any Medicare claim that health care provider organizations determine if beneficiaries have other coverage that would be primary to Medicare. Failure to do so can lead to allegations of fraud. Whether Medicare is primary or secondary should be determined at the point of service by patient access services employees. Front-end registration employees must complete the re-

quired Medicare secondary payer (MSP) questionnaire with Medicare beneficiaries. In general, Medicare is secondary if:
- patients work for an employer with 20 or more employees
- patients require medical care due to workers' compensation or other third-party liability situations, such as traffic accidents
- patients are disabled Medicare enrollees currently covered by an employer-provider health care plan or as a family member of an employee with benefits through his or her employer

Medicaid

This is a combined federal and state program to provide health care for individuals living below the poverty line. Again, Medicaid embraces managed care, with the most current data showing that more than 40 percent of the nation's Medicaid beneficiaries are enrolled in Medicaid managed care plans.

TRICARE/CHAMPUS

The Civilian Health and Medical Program of the Uniformed Services (CHAMPUS) is a federal indemnity insurance program providing coverage for military dependents, retirees and their dependents, and certain others, for hospital and medical services beyond that available in military treatment facilities.

Since CHAMPUS, additional TRICARE contracts have been established with insurers who agree to provide managed care for these beneficiaries. The coverage options include traditional indemnity, which is called TRICARE Standard or traditional CHAMPUS. TRICARE Prime is the HMO version, and TRICARE Extra offers PPO-like coverage.

Commercial Plans

Payers in the commercial market offer a bevy of health plan options, from traditional indemnity or fee-for-service plans absent any risk-sharing requirements, to various managed care plans in which risk is shared with providers and/or employers.

Managed Care

The design of and requirements under managed care health plans are in a constant state of refinement. Included among managed care plan offerings are:
- health maintenance organizations (HMOs), in which services are provided in return for a fixed, paid premium and under which provider choice is limited
- preferred provider organizations (PPOs), in which enrollees gain larger choice of primary and specialty care providers with fewer utilization restrictions than an HMO has (Unlike HMOs, a PPO will pay for services provided by noncontracted providers, albeit at lower reimbursement rates.)
- point-of-service (POS) plans, in which enrollees typically retain the ability to choose a participating or nonparticipating provider, with corresponding benefit or "penalty" of copay depending upon the level of benefit selected

PATIENTS ARE A NETTLESOME PAYER TYPE

Regardless of the plan type, virtually all require that patients pay a portion of their health care bill, through premiums as well as through a deductible and/or copayments. Although some level of patient-pay obligations are now the norm, it remains common for patients to act surprised, feign ignorance, or otherwise be unprepared to pay their portion for health care services. There is a growing emphasis for patient access employees to collect these self-pay balances up front, at the time of service.

However, because of the ongoing need for patient education to change a persistent, decades-old presumption and expectation of full insurance coverage, outstanding self-pay balances are a significant problem in accounts receivable management. Highlighting this problem is the fact that patient-pay balances comprise an average of 5.3 percent of total gross revenue among the nation's hospitals yet account for nearly 15 percent of total accounts receivable. The chapter on standard collection tips provides advice on tackling collection of patient-pay balances.

IT ALL STARTS UP FRONT

The most effective collection efforts rely on a close tie-in with the patient access services department. Registration and admissions employees set the pace for collections based on the accuracy and completeness of the registration record. Critical data obtained at registration will determine the collectablility of accounts.

It is not uncommon for collectors to blame registration for problems encountered during collection follow-up due to missing or inaccurate demographic or financial data gathered on the front end. However, it behooves collectors to take proactive steps to correct these problems rather than merely complain. It is important to provide positive feedback on resolving troublesome issues that frustrate collection attempts due to poor data quality when the patient record was initiated at registration.

Many facilities opt to have collectors shadow registration representatives and vice versa so that each receives first-hand experience and working knowledge of the link between the two areas. Some facilities also cross-train employees to bolster understanding between the departments and break down some of the adversarial barriers that may exist. Importantly, by pairing patient access with collections employees, front-end employees gain insight on just how crucial it is for registration data to be accurate and thorough to enable collectors to obtain reimbursement and, thus, sustain the financial viability of the institution.

And there is some give and take that can and should take place. For instance, collectors can serve as mentors in the realm of up-front collections by providing advice, feedback, and guidance as front-end employees pursue time-of-service collections of patient-pay balances.

Time-of-service collections is an important element in an effective collection strategy that pays off in reduced accounts receivable, improved cash flow, and, thus, improved gross days revenue outstanding (GDRO). However, nearly a third of hospitals don't even attempt to collect from patients at the time of service, and only 18 percent of hospitals consistently seek payment from patients at the time of service.

Those that do rely on the front-end employees as members of the collections team see results in the bottom line. Hospital survey data shows that facilities that make the greatest effort to collect from patients at the time of service also have the lowest GDRO average. Not surprisingly, at facilities where time-of-service collections is not a priority, the reverse is true, as GDRO escalates.

The disparity in GDRO performance between hospitals that diligently pursue up-front collections and those that do not is not surprising. A key reason is that payment requests made at the time of service are directed to patients. Once patients leave your facility, they are debtors, a far more difficult pool of people to collect from, as any collector will attest.

The patient vs. debtor distinction is critical. Patients are more inclined and have greater incentives to pay prior to or at the time of service, when the link between medical services and fees is greatest. The urgency to pay for health care diminishes significantly once patients receive the service and leave the facility.

When collectors align with front-end employees, it is important that it occur in a constructive manner. To improve collection effectiveness with the aid of patient access services, try these steps:

- Identify health plan contractual requirements that must be met up front and provide this data to patient access staff.
- Track the reasons for rebills, payment delays, and denials, and identify those linked to the quality of data gathered on the front end. Share this information with patient access services managers and employees so that they can improve processes to eradicate problems that cost the facility lost dollars because of claim delays and denials. Four areas to look at include the following:
  1. Are Medicare denials a problem due to ineffective MSP screening, which would reveal an insurer that is primary to Medicare?
  2. Are insurance data accurate and complete, or are patient records that are moving to the back end lacking sufficient in-

formation about the patient's insurer, group number, identification number, policy number, or the subscriber's name?
3. Are managed care claims delayed or denied due to failure to meet contractual preauthorization or precertification requirements prior to or at the time of service?
4. Is the facility incurring losses under Medicare due to failure to obtain ABNs from patients at the time of service?

- Meet with front-end employees at least quarterly to develop a dialogue and collaborate on problems that require resolution by front-end staff.

A coordinated effort that brings all forces to bear, starting with the front end, is an important step to developing and honing timely and effective collection efforts.

BEING A PEST IS A GOOD THING — WITH CAVEATS INCLUDED

Timely collections follow-up not only improves collection success, it also may garner for collectors the label of pest, both of which are positive outcomes. Payers of any type who are hounded by courteous yet persistent collectors typically will want to make them go away, and the only way to do so is to pay up.

The emphasis must be on professional courtesy, however. A good collector is not only persistent, but lets payers know their efforts to resolve issues to get a claim paid are appreciated. Effective collections requires developing a relationship with payers, an endeavor that transforms the ordinary collections pest into an appreciative collections professional. And an appreciative "pest" will always get better results.

HUMAN RELATIONS SKILLS ARE A CRITICAL COLLECTIONS TOOL

While collectors must have a depth of technical knowledge to pursue reimbursement from government and commercial payers, as well as from patients, human relations skills are perhaps among the most important. The ability to work with people, create a sense of urgency, and motivate others to not only promise to pay but also make good on those promises requires sophisticated communication skills.

Developing and nurturing a relationship with major payers is one of surest ways to step up claims turnaround times and ensure accurate payments. Communicate with these payers routinely on a friendly basis. Health care provider organizations may indeed be customers of insurance carriers, but these payers will be more inclined to carry out good customer service if the customer is calm, rational, and polite while still being persistent. There is no reason to be combative. Rather, be consistent and firm in collections follow-up to gain cooperation and consideration from payers.

To nurture good relations with payers, follow these ideas:

- **Ask what you can do for them.**

    For example, when following up to inquire about when payment will be made on a claim, refrain from simply demanding payment. Instead, ask if there is anything you can do to speed reimbursement.

- **Follow through.**

    This works both ways. If a payer representative indicates that more information is needed, and you promise to fax it within the hour, do so. Then, follow through to learn if the representative received the information and whether further information is required. Or, if a payer representative states he will investigate the claim status by Friday, call on Friday to learn the outcome.

    Such follow-through is important so that payers learn that you will do as you say and that you will follow up on what they say. It is a marketing technique as much as it is a tool to develop a good business relationship. Make good on your promises to deliver required information by a specified time or date, and you can ask for the same follow-through and consideration from payers.

    Key to effective follow-through is to remain in contact with the person responsible for adjudicating the claim. When speaking with a payer representative, be sure to ask for his or her name and confirm that the person you are speaking with is indeed the appropriate person to handle resolution and payment of the claim.

- **Show your appreciation.**

When third-party payer representatives are responsive and helpful, be sure to thank them. Every time you are on the telephone with a payer representative, you have gained something, even if it wasn't the desired result. You may learn that the claim isn't in the system, that it is slated for denial, or that it won't be paid until there is a full month of Sundays. Still, you have gained necessary knowledge to craft your follow-up strategy and gain reimbursement. Thus, the words "thank you" should be a routine part of your closing comments.

Showing your appreciation is particularly critical if someone goes out of his or her way to clear up a problem account. In such cases, sending a personal thank-you note, a letter of commendation to his or her supervisor (with a copy to the employee as well), chocolates, flowers, or some other show of appreciation is very appropriate. Keep in mind, a $25 flower arrangement now and again is a small investment to improve turnaround times on claims that contribute hundreds and thousands of dollars to the facility's bottom line.

CLEAN CLAIMS COME FIRST

The most troublesome element in the collection process is the issue of clean claims. There is no standard definition of the phrase, yet it is one that often presents as an obstacle to reimbursement. For effective collections follow-up, however, clean claims are a must.

This is more science than art when it comes to government payers, as clean claims hinge on meeting requirements defined by state and federal agencies. While these requirements and their nuances are in a constant state of flux and the details of the requirements, exclusions, and regulations are extensive, experts in government payers have a body of information — albeit a massive body of information — upon which they can rely.

Commercial payers, and managed care payers in particular, present a different and significant challenge. Contracts with these payer organizations are far from standard. Requirements vary by contract and it is critical for collectors to be aware of the varying contractual obligations and requirements for commercial and managed care payers.

Further complicating collections from commercial carriers is the fact that the emphasis within these payers seems to be on selling their health plan products to employers and enrollees rather than on servicing those contracts with providers. Another common lament among health care collectors is the lack of sophisticated systems and infrastructure for payers themselves to track and adjudicate claims according to the contractual agreement. Payers have built complexity into their contracts without building in the systems necessary to effectively manage and service that complexity in their partnerships with providers.

Electronic data interchange (EDI) is a case in point. While studies have shown that EDI is a win-win-win for providers, patients, and payers, with projected savings surpassing $9 billion a year, commercial payers have been slow to get in line for this technological improvement and lag behind government payers.

In addition to operational cost savings, electronic claims processing should, in theory, improve turnaround time for receivables. That has been the case with Medicare and Medicaid, or Title XIX, accounts. Receivables from these government payers typically turn around within two weeks, given a clean claim.

In contrast, fewer than 30 percent of commercial carriers have systems in place to allow for electronic claims processing in many markets. This failure to embrace EDI not only severely diminishes the ability to reap significant savings among providers and payers alike, it takes a huge toll on providers alone.

This is seen in gross revenue and total accounts receivable data by payer type. In the first quarter 2000, hospitals reported that nearly 43 percent of gross revenue came from Medicare, with about 24 percent of outstanding accounts receivable tied to Medicare, indicating a speedier turnaround time due to electronic claims processing. In contrast, managed care comprised nearly 27 percent of total gross revenue as well as nearly 25 percent of total accounts receivable.[1] These and other percentages are shown in the following table:

Payer Type	Total Percent of Gross Revenue	Total Percent of Accounts Receivable
Medicare	42.9%	24.2%
Medicaid	9.7%	11.2%
Commercial	10.4%	15.1%
Managed care	26.6%	24.6%

PAYER COLLECTION STRATEGIES

There are several key strategies to effectively collect from any third-party payer — government, commercial, or patient — as well as some special techniques for each. First, a look at eight key collection strategies common to any payer type:

1. **Use the telephone.**

    This may sound obvious, but it is important to emphasize human contact rather than relying on written follow-up through collection letters and related correspondence. Attempting telephone contact can be frustrating if the collector is put on hold or if the representative seems never to be available. However, once a collector finally does connect with a payer, the results are specific and immediate. For instance, if the payer says the claim is "pending," the collector can immediately inquire about what is needed to move the claim beyond pending status, and then can immediately take the action required to secure payment.

2. **Be knowledgeable.**

    Ongoing education is critical for collectors and a strong working knowledge of specific payer requirements is imperative. Because complexity continues to mount with all payer types, specialization is becoming the norm and specialized education is mandatory. For example, collectors who focus on managed care accounts need access to those contracts to knowledgeably work accounts and combat payment delays and denials. Employees who specialize in Medicare need a different body of knowledge, one that is constantly evolving. Education is absolutely critical for collection success.

3. **Stay upbeat and positive.**

    A sure route to collection defeat is a negative attitude. Stay upbeat and positive when investigating why a claim has not been paid. Remember, there is nothing wrong with seeking payment for services rendered. It is common business practice in every other industry. Unlike other industries, however, payment denials in health care are rampant. A good attitude will take a collector a long way toward correctly identifying the reason a payment is delayed or withheld, and what it will take to jump-start the account and gain reimbursement.

    Regardless of whether the collector believes payment delays or denials are inappropriate or intentional, the collector should steer clear of leveling accusations or debating the merit of a claim. Instead, stay focused on the collections mission — to identify what is needed, and then provide it, to obtain payment.

4. **Create a sense of urgency.**

    Delayed or denied payments hurt cash flow, which hurts a provider's ability to extend health care, make payroll, or buy materials and supplies. Any number of negative consequences may result from delayed or denied reimbursement. A good collector will convey a sense of urgency by underscoring the reliance upon timely and accurate payments to ensure the provider remains a viable organization that is able to serve the payer's clients.

5. **Know your accounts and thoroughly document collection activity.**

    Detailed account information must be at a collector's fingertips during follow-up with insurance representatives and patients. Having this information is critical so that a collector is prepared to respond to any objection a payer might have to processing a claim for payment.

    For instance, if the insurer states the claim was never received, a collector with detailed account information can state when the claim was submitted. Then, follow up immediately with an offer to fax a copy of the missing claim, and call back to ensure the fax was received.

Detailed documentation of collection activity also must be maintained to effectively manage an account, ensure the same ground isn't covered repeatedly, and effectively fight denials. For instance, if a payer fails to pay within mandated deadlines and the case escalates to review by the state insurance commissioner or other authority, a collector needs documentation to show that efforts to provide needed information to obtain reimbursement were made within the required time frame.

6. **Keep detailed account notes.**

   In addition to detailed documentation of account activity, the collector should document the names, telephone numbers, dates, and times of every collection call, as well as the action taken or required. This information is valuable in helping collectors remain up to speed on the status of collection activity. Plus, it opens the door to meeting the critical need of building relationships. Continued follow-up with the same insurance representative allows for continuity during the collections life of a claim and reduces time wasted in reviewing collection activity with a different insurance representative.

   Note: In addition, detailed documentation of collection activity is needed to identify recurrent problems in obtaining payment. These problems may stem from outdated chargemasters or ineffective registration practices, for example, or from problems with contracts with specific payers. Detailed collections account activity reports will surface consistent problems or errors so that education can take place where needed or so that renegotiation can be initiated to resolve those issues and eliminate problems.

7. **Develop key contacts.**

   As a collector becomes familiar with various insurance representatives, some representatives will rise to the top as being the most knowledgeable and/or most willing to help. Keep tabs on these people so that you can turn to them first when pursuing collections on future claims with the same carrier. Again, relationships matter.

8. **Be willing to appeal to a higher authority.**

The higher authority might be a supervisor, the patient, an employer, or the state insurance commissioner. Contacting patients and employers is among the most effective strategies, because these are an insurer's key customers as they are paying for the health plan product.

The key is to communicate to payer representatives the reason for the appeal in a positive manner rather than wielding it as a threat. It should be a simple statement of fact: "I'm sorry, but it appears nonpayment would be in violation of our contract with your firm. Since we are unable to work together to remedy this situation, I'll need to take this up with Mrs. Patient and her employer. Thank you."

In many cases, the payer representative may suddenly find there is something he or she can do to process the claim and preempt the need for providers to call upon patients or employers to intervene.

COLLECTION STRATEGIES BY PAYER TYPE

In addition to relying upon the above strategies to collect on accounts from payers that have received a clean bill from a provider organization, other collection strategies can be used for specific payer types. These additional strategies for specific payers contain collection principles that naturally cross over and can apply to other payers. However, there are some subtle and not so subtle nuances involved in collecting from government and commercial payers.

Commercial and Managed Care Payers

According to first quarter 2000 data, commercial and managed care payers comprise 37 percent of hospitals' gross revenue and about 40 percent of hospitals' accounts receivable.[2]

Although many contracts specify that the insurer will pay within 30 to 45 days, commercial insurers often are far off the promised payment mark. Knowledge is the greatest tool working in a collector's favor to secure payment from commercial and managed care payers. Collectors must have a solid working knowledge of a payer's contract to effectively extract reimbursement according to contractual requirements. In many cases, astute collectors may find they may know more about contract rules, requirements, and obligations than the payer representative.

In addition, effective collection strategies with commercial and managed care payers include the following:

- **Determine why the claim hasn't been paid.**

    Don't settle for excuses such as, "The claim is pending," or, "It's under review." Those statements are the same as, "I don't know why we haven't paid you." Although the payer representative may indeed not know why a claim is held up, this person should ferret out that information. Verify the billing date and the date the claim was received, and then be persistent in finding out specifics about why the claim hasn't been paid. (Be sure to track the excuses for future reference in working with the payer to prevent denials before they occur.) Determine if further information is needed and, if so, provide it.

- **Ask for payment.**

    If there is no additional action required by the provider and no further information is requested, ask when payment can be expected. If the representative is unable to provide a date for payment, request to speak with a supervisor.

- **Contact the employer if collection attempts fail with no adequate explanation for delay or denial of payment.**

    Employers are frustrated with the high cost of health care benefits for employees. Given the huge expense of health care, they expect health plans to follow through with good service for their employees. The last person a managed care plan wants to hear from is a disgruntled employee benefits manager who is fielding complaints from providers and patients about the plan's refusal to pay for services.

    Note: Don't be afraid to alert health plan representatives to the fact that you plan to contact the employer. This alert may be enough to prod them into action. If not, there is no reason to

keep it secret, nor should it be used as a threat. As always, it is important to remain professional and polite. Stating that you will be contacting the employer simply informs the health plan of your next step.
- **Understand contracts.**

  Many managed care contracts have a timely payment clause that requires payment within a 30-day or 45-day window. Don't expect anything less. In fact, while penalty clauses are not yet the norm, some states do level penalties against slow-paying health plans. For providers that hold contracts with penalty clauses, a simple statement like, "I'm sure you would like to avoid having the interest penalty clause kick in, so what do we need to do to get this claim paid and avoid potential interest fees for your firm?" can be effective in securing payment.
- **Seek educational opportunities with payers.**

  A tour of payer offices can be a good way to learn about claims processing from the other side. It is also effective to request that a payer representative meet with collectors to provide an overview and background on the claims processing process. This not only creates a foundation for a better hands-on working knowledge of payer practices, it also helps forge relationships with payers.

Medicaid and Medicare

Medicaid often is described as the most difficult payer from which a collector seeks to eke out payment. Effective collections follow-up requires zeroing in on the reason a claim is denied — it may be a simple transposition of digits within a code — and identifying the remedy to remove the obstacle to payment. A common lament is that Medicaid employees seem unwilling or unable to help. Be persistent in seeking referral to a supervisor, repeatedly if necessary, until you are connected with someone who can deliver results.

A similar strategy should be used in pursuing collections on Medicare accounts. In addition, consider the following:
- **Keep current with updates.** As noted earlier, these programs seem to be a constant state of flux. It is important for billing

and claims processing requirements to be communicated to collectors and billing staff. Medicare offers programs to help train provider employees on the Medicare program and requirements for compliance and payment.
- **Enter remittance advices promptly.** The remittance advice, which spells out why claims have not been paid, must be entered promptly to avoid needlessly following up on appropriately denied claims.
- **Review for coding accuracy.** Coding inaccuracy is a key reason Medicare claims turn up on a collector's work list. It is important for physicians to work closely with the medical records department to ensure the most accurate code is used. This code must prove medical necessity, a vague term that often is used when denying claims. While excluded Medicare services are clearly outlined, covered services are not, with most covered under the broad label of "medically necessary" services.
- **Be willing and ready to appeal.** The appeals process may be contained at the carrier level, or it may need to be escalated to the highest level: federal court review. There are minimum claims account balance levels for the five appeal levels within Medicare, as well as filing requirements. Appeals are costly, so carefully evaluate payment reductions and denials to determine the likelihood of success upon appeal. When an analysis shows the denial or reduction was in error and an appeal will likely be in your favor, pursue it.

TRICARE/CHAMPUS

While claims for the U.S. Department of Defense program of managed care, TRICARE, and CHAMPUS fall into the small "other" category of hospital receivables, it is a category that requires diligence to ensure payment. Some collectors rely upon a "deluge of information" method to collect from TRICARE, providing any and all information about a claim to prevent denials.

Some tips to speed payment follow:

- **Provide a copy of the patient's identification card.** The card is important as it includes the name of the base at which the patient is stationed, and sometimes the base will cover the expense through TRICARE.
- **Include all information related to the patient and claim in follow-up efforts.** This information, obtained from medical records, should include a pathology report, physician's first report, emergency department notes, and other information related to the services provided, as well as consultation reports and/or narratives.
- **Submit the original claim.** If there is no response within 90 days, send a status request. This request simply states that there has been a lack of response and asks for advice on the status.
- **Ensure the proper billing form is used.** TRICARE typically denies claims submitted on improper billing forms, making it imperative for collectors to verify that the HCFA 1500 or the UB-92 submitted with a claim was indeed the proper billing form.
- **Verify the claim for completeness, particularly in code numbers and modifiers.** Medical records is the coding source for matching procedures with accurate codes, but collectors must ensure that the HCPCS, ICD-9, and CPT-4 codes required to process the claim are indeed on the claim. If accuracy of codes is questioned, then collectors must return to medical records to clarify and remedy inaccurate coding issues.
- **Ensure block 31 on the TRICARE claim is initialed.** Failure to initial this block will result in denial.
- **Ensure the sponsor's Social Security number is used when submitting a claim, not the patient's if the patient is a spouse of a member of the armed services.**
- **Do not attempt to file claims of active duty armed services patients to TRICARE.** These claims must be sent to the specific branch of service — the U.S. Army, Navy, Air Force, or Marines.
- **Understand CHAMPUS and TRICARE requirements.** The most effective collection tool is knowledge that can be used to prevent payment delays and denials.

Workers' Compensation

While this payer type also falls into the small "other" category of receivables, it can be riddled with time-consuming problems. Standards and requirements vary by state, and when problems arise, resolving these cases can be long, drawn-out affairs.

To effectively tackle workers' compensation claims, be sure to do the following:

- **Verify that the injury or illness is work related** by contacting the employer, and verify that the employee is covered by workers' compensation insurance. Not all employees are covered by a workers' compensation policy. Part-time employees or independent contractors, for instance, may not be covered. Plus, employers in some states are not required to cover employees.
- **Ensure that first report of injury has been submitted.** If this report is not on file, contact the employer and request that it be sent via fax so that you can follow up with the insurer.
- **Verify the billing address.**
- **Recruit physicians** to write a letter of appeal if denial is based on lack of medical necessity.
- **Ensure thorough documentation of the account history.** Documenting account history is critical for collections follow-up on workers' compensation claims because of the nature of the account and the fact that multiple parties may be involved to resolve claim disputes and determine the liable party.
- **Know your state laws regarding workers' compensation.**

PATIENTS AS ALLIES

Regardless of payer type, patients are key allies as collectors seek payment from problem payers. Patients with insurance coverage, be it through an employer-sponsored plan, a government agency, or workers' compensation, expect that coverage will protect them from incurring significant financial liability for health care services. Thus, patients can become a collector's key ally in tackling objections to payment because patients don't want to see the claim dumped in their lap.

In the case of CHAMPUS claims, for example, patients often are able to serve as a liaison to help get an account cleared up as they know who to contact on their base.

For workers' compensation claims, again, patients are key allies in ensuring the needed information is obtained from employers and physicians so that workers' compensation coverage kicks in to the fullest extent possible.

In working with government and commercial plans, patients hold clout because these payers place a premium on enrollee satisfaction. Managed care plans will be more responsive if patients become involved in inquiring about claim status. If claim issues are brought to the employer sponsoring the plan and the employer intervenes, again, payers take notice because a portion of their business may be at risk if claims are not resolved in a satisfactory manner and the employer disenrolls as a result.

When contacting patients to solicit their help in getting a claim paid, explain the situation and provide details about the status of the account. If you have submitted the claim for payment five times, let patients know. If the payer has requested additional information and you have provided it, and still you have not received payment, explain this to patients.

Don't exaggerate, but be clear and provide details about the difficulties encountered in gaining payment. And emphasize your desire to resolve the issue so that it doesn't become the patient's responsibility.

Here is a sample dialogue:

"Hello, Mrs. Smith. This is Mrs. Tim with ABC Hospital. I'm calling because we are having trouble obtaining payment from your insurer for services you received at our facility. I'm sure you pay your premiums on time, and it doesn't seem fair that your insurer isn't as responsive in paying your claim. I wouldn't want you to have to pay for these services, and I was hoping you might contact your insurer to inquire about why they are failing to pay for the services."

The collector then would explain the difficulties encountered and provide the patient with a name and contact number for the insurer.

Another option is to offer to put the patient on a conference call with you and the insurer. Such a three-way conversation often speeds payment as payers are unlikely to be vague or evasive when their client is on the telephone. Plus, patients might prefer to have you on the line as the expert on the status of the account. Conference calls also work in the collector's favor because the patient's conversation with the payer is less likely to turn into a he-said-she-said affair, requiring repeated callbacks if questions arise that the patient or the payer is unable to answer.

Although some contracts stipulate that patients cannot be contacted for payment on denied claims, there is no reason a collector cannot contact patients to gain their help and cooperation in getting a claim paid. Plus, there is an argument that if payers refuse to pay according to contract, then the validity of the contract is in question and billing patients is fair game. Legal advice should be sought in cases with gray areas about whether patients can be billed for denied charges.

CONCLUSION

Health care collections is becoming increasingly complex, requiring that collectors seek and receive ongoing education about government and commercial payers and their related contracts, rules, regulations, and requirements. The complexity of today's contracts with payers places additional pressure on health care collectors because it is not uncommon for the payers themselves to be unaware of contractual obligations or what the payment is supposed to be.

Collections follow-up must be proactive to the greatest extent possible to prevent payment delays, reductions, or denials. Health care collectors should initiate contact with payers early in the process rather than waiting for and reacting to payers' responses. In addition, collectors must review payments to ensure that the payer reimbursed the provider at the proper level. If not, further follow-up is required to reverse denials or reductions in payment on claims.

Although health care collections is replete with change, one constant remains: the need for excellent human relations and communication skills. Such skills remain as one of the most critical complements to a strong working knowledge of payer requirements. Health care collectors must be personable and professional, knowledgeable and persistent.

It goes back to the old adage, "The squeaky wheel gets the grease." In health care collections, the doggedly persistent and eminently professional collector gets paid.

REFERENCES

1. *HARA (Hospital Accounts Receivable Analysis)*, first quarter 2000 (Gaithersburg, MD: Aspen Publishers, Inc.).
2. *HARA (Hospital Accounts Receivable Analysis)*, first quarter 2000.

SUGGESTED READING

The Managed Care Payment Advisor, Vol. 2, No. 1 (July 1998).

HARA (Hospital Accounts Receivable Analysis), first quarter 2000 (Gaithersburg, MD: Aspen Publishers, Inc.).

Patient Account Manager's 1999 Sourcebook (Gaithersburg, MD: Aspen Publishers, Inc.).

R. Rognehaugh, *The Managed Health Care Dictionary, Second Edition* (Gaithersburg, MD: Aspen Publishers, Inc., 1998).

SOURCE CONSULTED

James N. Struck, president, Mutual Hospital Services Inc., Indianapolis, Ind., and executive director of the National Healthcare Collectors Association.

CHAPTER 4

Sample Collection Letters

Collection letters need to be as effective as possible in terms of both collection results and public relations. This can be a hard combination to maintain, since many patients would argue the best public relations policy a hospital could have would be to disregard all debts owed by patients.

This chapter includes a variety of collection letters that have been field tested with great success, as well as tips for writing effective letters of your own.

Collection letters should be reviewed at least once a year to keep them up-to-date. Use the following checklist to review your collection letters and notices:

- Are they short and to the point? Letters should be one page with short paragraphs and brief sentences.
- Look for words that may confuse your reader. Avoid technical jargon that your patients may not understand.
- Review your first paragraph. This is the attention-getter and must be designed to keep the patient reading. Do not provoke anger.
- Remove any "we expect" or "we need" statements that will turn off the reader.
- Be specific about a time frame for payment.

- Make sure your letter gives a reason for the patient to do what you are asking.
- Personalize the letter when possible. Have it signed by an individual and avoid saying "Dear Patient."
- Include payment options in every letter such as credit card or bank financing.
- Make sure your letter provides a way for patients to contact you (address and phone number).

Tip: Use collection letters on accounts with relatively large balances. Such letters are expensive compared to other efforts and often do not get the results you're looking for, so they should not be relied upon as a primary collection tool. Make collection efforts by phone first.

HOW TO WRITE A COLLECTION LETTER

The following two letters show what makes a bad letter bad and how to make it better.

(Instructional comments are in italic within parentheses.)

Sample Collection Letters 55

Before

> Date: 7/5/00
> *(Printing the wrong date is a common error, particularly in the beginning of a new year or new month. Also, write the date, spelling out the month and the complete year.)*
>
> Patient's Name: Bill Brown
> *(Use the patient's full name, not a nickname.)*
> Address: 2175 Pondwater Court
>   Kelp, VA 27502
>
> Account #: 123456789
>
> Balance Due: $350.00
>
>
> Dear Mr. Brawn:
> *(Always check the spelling of even the simplest names. Patients may get very upset when their names are misspelled, lowering your chance of payment.)*
> When you came to *(poor sentence structure)* Owitch Medical Center, you were orientated *(The word "orientated" is often misused. In this case, "oriented" is the proper word. "Orientated" means "to face East.")* about our payment policies upon registration. Was there a problem with the bill? *(Never ask if there was a problem. It encourages the patient to think of one.)* You have already avoided *(This sounds far too harsh and would likely make the patient defensive.)* two collection letters and a series of calls from this office.
> Despite our efforts, we haven't received a payment from you yet. You must pay immediately or the account will be given to a collection agency. *(This doesn't sound too threatening, so it may not have any effect on the patient.)*
> If your *(This is the wrong word, but most spell checkers won't catch the error.
> The proper word is "you're.")* unable to completely fulfill your obligation for making payment to our facility, you must contact me directly.
> Phone number should have been included here.
> Its *(Again, the wrong word is used. "It's" is correct here.)* imperative for you to address this issue immediately. *(Give a deadline by which the patient must reach you before further action is taken.)*
>
> Sincerely,
> Betty Adams *(Give your full name and title.)*

After

July 5, 2000

Patient's Name: William Brown
Address: 2175 Pondwater Court
Kelp, VA 27502

Account #: 123456789

Balance Due: $350.00

Dear Mr. Brown:

Your bill is 60 days past due.

Prior to being treated at our facility, you agreed to accept the terms of our payment policy. We have yet to receive payment from you for services we provided in good faith. Is there anything I can do to help you meet your financial obligation?

In most instances, when a bill is more than 60 days past due the matter is immediately turned over to a collection agency, often damaging the patient's credit rating. We have delayed this action to give you a final opportunity to settle this account.

This delay will not last forever, though. If payment is not sent within 10 days of receipt of this letter, I will have no choice but to send your account to an agency.

Mr. Brown, it's important that you take care of this matter immediately. Please contact me today so we can arrange payment. You can contact me directly at 201 555-1234.

Sincerely,

Elizabeth Adams
Collections Manager

P.S. For your convenience, we accept MasterCard, Visa, and Discover.

SAMPLE COLLECTION LETTERS

The following letters are written for a variety of circumstances. The typical use for each letter is listed, but you may find ways to rewrite them for other uses (i.e., rewriting a payer-specific letter for use as a patient reminder letter.)

Letters to Patients

[Patient Balance Final Demand]

September 1, 2000

Paul Kleinstadt
1071 Ocean Blvd.
Niceville, FL 00015

RE: Account #: 12345678

FINAL NOTICE

Dear Paul:

Your <u>Memorial Hospital</u> account balance of $_____ remains unpaid to date, despite previous requests for payment. We have exhausted all attempts to settle your debt.

Please send a check payable to <u>Memorial Hospital</u>. If your full payment of $____ is not received within seven (7) days of receipt of this letter then I will be obligated to refer your account to an outside collection agency.

Please avoid such action and remit your payment of $____ to <u>Memorial Hospital</u> TODAY using the payment stub and self addressed, stamped envelope enclosed. *VISA, MASTERCARD, and DISCOVER* cards are accepted.

If you have any questions regarding this account, please contact me at _____. Thank you in advance for your cooperation.

Sincerely,

Rebekah Kowalchek
Reimbursement Specialist

[Patient Claim Form Needed/Enclosed]

September 1, 2000

Paul Kleinstadt
1071 Ocean Blvd.
Niceville, FL 00015

RE: Account #: 12345678

INSURED: Kleinstadt, Paul
EMPLOYER: Niceville Helium, Inc.
SOCIAL SECURITY #: 123456789

Dear Paul:

We have submitted claims to your insurance carrier on your behalf for services rendered by <u>Memorial Hospital</u>. Recently, your insurance company advised us that they will not consider payment until they receive a claim form completed by the insured.

Please complete the enclosed claim form in full, and return it in the enclosed self-addressed envelope. Should I not receive this form **within ten (10) business days,** <u>Memorial Hospital</u> will be forced to bill you directly for services rendered. If you have any questions, please contact me at _____. Your prompt attention will be greatly appreciated.

Sincerely,

Rebekah Kowalchek
Reimbursement Specialist

Enclosure

[Inform Patient of Final Appeal]

September 1, 2000

Paul Kleinstadt
1071 Ocean Blvd.
Niceville, FL 00015

RE: Account #: 12345678

Balance: $

Dear Paul:

To date we have been unable to secure payment from your insurance company for the charges submitted on your behalf. The balance on your account is referenced above.

We are preparing a final appeal to your insurance company in an effort to overturn the denial of these charges. If this appeal is denied you could be held responsible for the above balance, or some portion thereof if prior arrangements have been made.

We would appreciate any assistance you can offer in dealing with your insurance company or employer in regards to their denial of these charges. Please contact me at _____ if you have any questions or need additional information.

Sincerely,

Rebekah Kowalchek
Reimbursement Specialist

[Inform Patient of Unsuccessful Appeal]

September 1, 2000

Paul Kleinstadt
1071 Ocean Blvd.
Niceville, FL 00015

RE: Account #: 12345678

Balance: $

Dear Paul:

I regret to inform you that all efforts have been exhausted in trying to appeal your insurance company's original "denied" status. On <u>August 28, 2000</u> our final appeal attempt was made without successful results.

Therefore, please continue to pay your monthly agreed upon payment amount of $ _____ on your balance.

Should you have any questions concerning the appeal process, please feel free to call me at _____. If you have any questions concerning your payment plan then please call your Financial Counselor at _____.

Sincerely,

Rebekah Kowalchek
Reimbursement Specialist

cc: Financial Counselor

[Insurance Company Denied/Need Additional Information from Patient]

September 1, 2000

Paul Kleinstadt
1071 Ocean Blvd.
Niceville, FL 00015

Dear Paul:

The claims recently submitted by <u>Memorial Hospital</u> to your insurance carrier have been returned for additional information. Please complete the information requested below, or call _____ to provide the information to us immediately upon receipt.

_____Copy of your medical record

_____Group number and/or policy number

_____Social Security number and/or ID number

_____Insured name

_____Employer name_____
          Address   _____
          City, State, ZIP _____
          Phone number _____

_____Coordination of benefits with other insurance

_____Other _____

Sincerely,

Rebekah Kowalchek
Reimbursement Specialist

[Insurance Company Denied/Bill Patient]

September 1, 2000

Paul Kleinstadt
1071 Ocean Blvd.
Niceville, FL 00015

RE: Account #: 12345678
Date(s) of Service: 4/18-4/20/2000
Charges: $
Service: Laparoscopy

Dear Paul:

After billing your insurance company on your behalf for the above referenced date(s) of service we received notification that the claim was not paid for the following reason(s):

_____Policy terminated
_____Policy has paid maximum benefits allowed
_____Other:_____

This letter is to inform you that due to the above reason checked you will be receiving a bill from <u>Memorial Hospital</u> for the above referenced date(s) of service and amount. This amount is now **your responsibility.**

We appreciate your prompt payment upon receiving our bill. Should you have any questions concerning this matter, please feel free to call me at _____.

Sincerely,

Rebekah Kowalchek
Reimbursement Specialist

[Settlement Letter]

September 1, 2000

Paul Kleinstadt
1071 Ocean Blvd.
Niceville, FL 00015

RE: Account #: 12345678
Account Balance: $
Settlement Amount: $

Dear Paul:

This letter is to follow up on our telephone conversation whereby I stated that receipt of the settlement amount referenced above by ____/____/____ will resolve your account balance in full. I appreciate your willingness to satisfy your obligation to <u>Memorial Hospital.</u>

Please complete the payment stub below, detach it, and mail it along with your payment using the self-addressed stamped envelope enclosed. Remember, we do accept *VISA, MASTERCARD, and DISCOVER* cards should this be a more convenient method of payment.

Thank you for your timely response to this settlement agreement. If you have any further questions, please feel free to contact me at _____.

Sincerely,

Rebekah Kowalchek
Reimbursement Specialist

PAYMENT STUB

ACCOUNT #: 12345678   *PATIENT NAME*: Paul Kleinstadt
Check One:

❑ Check or money order enclosed for $
❑ VISA   ❑ MASTERCARD   ❑ DISCOVER

Amount: $_____   Card #: _____

Cardholder Name: _____

Expiration Date: _____

Authorized Signature: _____

[Acknowledgment of Discount]

Paul Kleinstadt
1071 Ocean Blvd.
Niceville, FL 00015

RE: Account #: 123455678

Dear Paul:

As we discussed in our telephone conversation today, we estimate your portion of the charges will total $_____. Based on the information completed on the Financial Evaluation form, we agreed to a _____% discount on patient charges.

This discount will leave an estimated patient balance of $_____. We agreed that you would pay <u>Memorial Hospital</u> $ _____/month beginning ___/_____. Enclosed is a Payment Plan Agreement, if applicable. Should a Payment Plan Agreement be enclosed, then please sign and return it with your first payment. You may at any time pay your balance in full without penalty. This discount is contingent upon your timely monthly payments.

Should you have any questions, please feel free to call me at _____.

Sincerely,

Rebekah Kowalchek
Financial Counselor, Reimbursement Department

[Acknowledgment of Payment Plan]

Paul Kleinstadt
1071 Ocean Blvd.
Niceville, FL 00015

RE: Account #: 12345678

Date(s) of Service: 4/18-4/20/2000

PLAN AGREEMENT

Dear Paul,

As we discussed in our telephone conversation today, your account balance is $_____ for services rendered on the above referenced dates by Memorial Hospital. We appreciate the opportunity to have recently cared for you.

We have negotiated a **monthly payment** amount of $_____ beginning on _____/_____/_____. Please be advised that default on any scheduled payment will allow Memorial Hospital to demand full payment on the amount due immediately.

Please sign and return the enclosed original Payment Plan Agreement form with your first payment. Keep a copy for your records. A self-addressed, stamped envelope is enclosed for your convenience when making your first payment. A payment coupon booklet is also enclosed. Return one stub with each payment for proper credit to your account. Special stubs are included should you wish to make any of your payments with *VISA, MASTERCARD, OR DISCOVER* card. You may, **at any time**, pay your balance in full without penalty.

Should you have any questions, please feel free to call me at _____.

Sincerely,

Rebekah Kowalchek
Reimbursement Specialist

[Acknowledgment of Estimated Payment Plan]

MEMORIAL HOSPITAL
PAYMENT PLAN AGREEMENT

Patient's Name: Paul Kleinstadt
Account #: 123456768
Total Balance Due: $
Monthly Payment Amount: $
    First Payment Due: ___/___/____
    Final Payment Due: ___/___/____ Final Amount: $_____

Comments: _____

TERMS

1. ALL **PAYMENTS ARE DUE ON OR BEFORE YOUR** DUE DATE EACH MONTH.

2. This payment plan agreement will remain in effect, provided that the undersigned completes the agreed payment schedule upon the terms and conditions set forth herein. Upon default of any of the terms of this payment schedule, the original balance minus any payments shall become due immediately.

3. Failure to sign and return this document does not relieve the patient's obligation to this payment agreement of the balance noted above.

4. Memorial Hospital reserves the right to renegotiate the monthly payment amount at any time.

_____ _____
Signature of Patient/Responsible Party   Date

_____ _____
Printed Name of Patient/Responsible Party Date

_____ _____
Authorized Representative   Date

Please forward all payments to: Memorial Hospital
                                        1313 Mockingbird Lane
                                        Mainline, FL 20174

[Missed Payment Reminder]

September 1, 2000

Paul Kleinstadt
1071 Ocean Blvd.
Niceville, FL 00015

RE: Account #: 12345678

Dear Paul:

Our records indicate you missed your scheduled monthly payment of $_____, which was due on ____/____/____. As stated in the Payment Plan Agreement, all payments are due **on or before** your due date every month, and any default of such payment gives Memorial Hospital the right to request full payment immediately.

Please remit your payment of $_____ TODAY to avoid Memorial Hospital from requesting full payment of $_____. If, for some reason, you are unable to make this payment today, then please call me immediately at _____ to discuss an alternative arrangement.

A self-addressed, stamped envelope is enclosed for your convenience in making your payment today. Remember, we accept *VISA, MASTERCARD, and DISCOVER* cards, in which case you must complete the payment stub enclosed and return it to Memorial Hospital.

Sincerely,

Rebekah Kowalchek
Reimbursement Specialist

PAYMENT STUB

ACCOUNT #: 12345678   PATIENT NAME: Paul Kleinstadt
Check One:

❏ Check or money order enclosed for $
❏ VISA   ❏ MASTERCARD   ❏ DISCOVER
Amount: $_____   Card #: _____
Cardholder Name: _____
Expiration Date: _____
Authorized Signature: _____

[Missed Payment Plan Final Notice]

September 1, 2000

Paul Kleinstadt
1071 Ocean Blvd.
Niceville, FL 00015

RE: Account #: 12345678

Balance: $

FINAL NOTICE

Dear Paul:

On _____/_____/_____ I informed you that you missed your scheduled payment of $_____ and, to date, have still not received such payment. As per the terms of your Payment Plan Agreement, I am obligated to bill you for the full balance of your account since you have defaulted on monthly payment # _____.

Please remit the full balance of $_____ within **ten (10) days** of the date of this letter using the self-addressed, stamped envelope enclosed to avoid referral of your account to an outside collection agency. Should you need to discuss this matter, then please call me at _____.

Sincerely,

Rebekah Kowalchek
Reimbursement Specialist

cc: Department Manager

[Inform Patient of Insufficient Funds]

September 1, 2000

Paul Kleinstadt
1071 Ocean Blvd.
Niceville, FL 00015

RE: Check #: 671
Amount: $
Account #: 12345678

Dear Paul:

I regret to inform you that your check for $_____ made out to Memorial Hospital on ___/___/_____ has been **returned twice** by your bank for insufficient funds.

Your account has been debited for the amount referenced above, which will be reflected in your next monthly statement. Additionally, you will be charged a $20.00 returned check fee in accordance with our company policy.

Your total balance owed as of the date of this letter is $_____. Please remit in full using the enclosed self-addressed, stamped envelope and payment stub. We do accept *VISA, MASTERCARD, and DISCOVER* cards for your convenience. Just complete the appropriate section of the payment stub and return it to Memorial Hospital within fifteen (15) days of the date of this letter.

Thank you in advance for your prompt payment. Should you have questions, please feel free to call me at _____.

Sincerely,

Rebekah Kowalchek
Reimbursement Specialist

[Patient, Unable To Contact Re: Financial Obligation]

September 1, 2000

Paul Kleinstadt
1071 Ocean Blvd.
Niceville, FL 00015

RE: Account #: 123455678

Dear Paul:

<u>Memorial Hospital</u> appreciates the opportunity to care for you.

I have attempted to contact you by phone in order to discuss your financial obligation to <u>Memorial Hospital</u>. Please call me at your earliest convenience at _____. I would be glad to answer any questions concerning your insurance coverage, or amounts owed by you. I look forward to hearing from you soon.

Sincerely,

Rebekah Kowalchek
Financial Counselor

Letters to Third-Party Payers

[Correction Payment Error in Number of Days]

September 12, 2000

Dewey, Cheatem and Howe Insurance
2117 Dante Circle
Hales Corners, WI 53000
Attn: Claims Department

RE: Paul Kleinstadt
Subscriber: Paul Kleinstadt
Dates of Service: 4/18-4/20/2000
Policy #/Group #: 8675309
Account #: 112001

Dear Claims Department:

<u>Dewey, Cheatem and Howe</u> recently received payment for the above-referenced invoice, yet the number of service days paid does not match the number of days billed. Enclosed please find a copy of the claim and the explanation of benefits. Note that ___ days were paid, yet ___ days of service were provided and billed.

Please reprocess the enclosed claim **within the next** 30 days, and pay $____ for _____ additional days of service provided.

Should you have any questions concerning this request, please feel free to call me at _____. Thank you for your prompt response to this matter.

Sincerely,

Tom Shulman
Reimbursement Specialist

Enclosure

[Correction Underpayment]

September 12, 2000

Dewey, Cheatem and Howe Insurance
2117 Dante Circle
Hales Corners, WI 53000
Attn: Claims Department

Patient: Paul Kleinstadt
Insured: Paul Kleinstadt
Employer: Niceville Helium, Inc.
Policy #: 8675309
Social Security #: 112001

Dear Claims Department:

The claim submitted on behalf of the above-named patient for service dates of: 4/18-4/20/2000 has been processed incorrectly. Our charges reflected contract pricing; however, it appears that the claim was processed and paid below the contract pricing.

We request that you reprocess this claim according to the agreed contract pricing of $_____ per day for _____. For your review, we enclose a copy of the claim and a copy of the FOB received with payment.

Should you have any questions or if you need additional information, please contact me at _____.

Sincerely,

Tom Shulman
Reimbursement Specialist

[Appeal Partial Payment]

September 12, 2000

Dewey, Cheatem and Howe Insurance
2117 Dante Circle
Hales Corners, WI 53000
Attn: Claims Department

Patient: Paul Kleinstadt
Insured: Paul Kleinstadt
Employer: Niceville Helium, Inc.
Policy #: 8675309
Social Security #: 112001

Dear Claims Department:

We wish to appeal your denial of claims submitted on behalf of our patient named above, for services prescribed by <u>Dr. Walker</u>. In taking this patient on service, <u>Memorial Hospital</u> followed a standard protocol of insurance verification and clearance. Historically, we have received routine reimbursement from your company on patients with similar diagnosis and plan of treatment. For <u>Paul Kleinstadt</u> we only received partial payment from you.

If there has been a change in your policy concerning payment for these services, this has not been formally communicated to <u>Memorial Hospital</u>. If you have made a decision to change the eligibility of these services for coverage we would like notification so we can:
a) review our protocol and/or alter our clearance process prior to taking patients on service
b) make a fair and ethical decision with regard to whether or not to render care to our patients
However, until we receive notification, we can only operate in good conscience based on the expectation which you have given us by our past experience with your company.

We remain firm in our position that this care was rendered in good faith with fair and reasonable expectation for reimbursement based on the precedent which you have shown us, given that this patient has a diagnosis equivalent to significant numbers of previous patients for which claims were paid. Your retrospective denial (after performance of services;

continues

without prior notification to the provider) gives the appearance of an inconsistent application of benefits and unfair claim practices. This decision is clearly contradicted by the payments which we have already received for these services for this patient.

We urge you to reconsider our charges and trust this additional information will enable you to render a favorable decision. If you have any questions, please contact me at _____.

Sincerely,

Tom Shulman
Reimbursement Specialist

CHAPTER 5

Key Regulations

Several federal regulations govern the actions of health care collectors. Included in this chapter are summaries of these regulations, including a listing of the sections of the Fair Debt Collection Practices Act most relevant to health care collectors.

Note: This is not an exhaustive list of every law affecting collectors. In addition to these federal regulations, there are many state laws, which can be more stringent than those on the federal level. These laws can be found in *State-by-State Health Care Collection Laws and Regulations*, published by Aspen Publishers.

TRUTH IN LENDING CONSUMER CREDIT COST DISCLOSURE

Health care providers may legally charge interest on medical bills, even if the provider is a nonprofit facility. Even among providers who realize this, few take the opportunity to charge interest on medical bills because of the potential patient relations problems that could develop.

The Truth in Lending Consumer Credit Cost Disclosure requires businesses (including providers) to disclose all direct and indirect costs and conditions related to the granting of credit. Basically, anyone granting credit to a consumer is required to explain up front how much the credit will cost the consumer. All costs (interest, late charges, collection fees, finance charges, etc.) must be disclosed at or prior to the time of service.

If interest is being charged and the patient is billed each month, you must include the following information on all monthly statements:
- the amount of each payment
- payment due date
- unpaid balance at the beginning of the billing period
- finance charges
- date full balance is due

FAIR CREDIT REPORTING ACT

Credit reporting agencies who either issue or use reports on consumers in connection with the approval of credit are regulated by the Fair Credit Reporting Act. According to the Act, these agencies can only provide consumer reports when:
- given a court order to do so
- the consumer (patient) gives instruction to provide the report
- a person has a legitimate business need for the information

If a creditor, such as a provider, refuses credit to a patient based on a credit report, the reason credit was denied must be explained to the patient. The provider must also give the name and address of the credit agency from which the report came. If the report contains any inaccuracies, the patient has the opportunity to correct them.

FAIR CREDIT BILLING ACT

This law states that consumers (patients) have 60 days from the date a statement is mailed to complain about an error. Creditors (providers) must then acknowledge this complaint within 30 days of receiving it. If an actual error occurred, the provider is required to correct the mistake within two complete billing cycles — a maximum of 90 days. If the bill was accurate, the accuracy of the bill must be explained to the patient.

FAIR DEBT COLLECTION PRACTICES ACT

The federal Fair Debt Collection Practices Act (FDCPA) is the most well known and most powerful regulation affecting collectors. While collectors employed by a creditor, such as a hospital or clinic, are not specifically covered by the FDCPA, following the provisions of the Act will often ensure that collectors comply with state regulations, which often mirror those of the FDCPA.

Because the FDCPA is extremely long and complex, clarified summaries of the key passages are included below, followed by the original text of those sections of the Act.

Telephone Collection Guidelines

The FDCPA provides the following eight guidelines for telephone collection:
1. Debtors may only be contacted once per day. Calls cannot be made before 8 a.m. or after 9 p.m. in the debtor's time zone.
2. Contacting a debtor on a Sunday, or any other day that the debtor recognizes as a Sabbath, could be considered harassment.
3. Repeated calls in one day could be considered harassment, even if a debtor has asked the collector to call back. In some states, harassment could be cited if more than one contact attempt was made in the same week.
4. The debtor should only be contacted at work if the debtor cannot be contacted in any other way. Collectors may not attempt to contact the debtor at work if the debtor's employer doesn't allow phone calls.
5. You may not call a debtor repeatedly, or let the phone ring with the intent to annoy.
6. Collectors must identify themselves and the organization they represent. The collector cannot give the debtor any personal information.

7. If the debtor is represented by an attorney, all contact must be made through that attorney. The collector can only contact the debtor directly if the attorney does not respond.
8. If written notification is received to discontinue calls to the debtor, all communication must stop. The collector is allowed one final call to advise the debtor that collection has stopped, or that legal action has been taken.

Illegal Methods

Collectors may not:
- threaten to harm a debtor physically or by reputation
- use obscene or profane language
- publish lists of debtors who refuse to pay, unless such lists are being sent to a credit reporting agency
- make calls without identifying themselves

The law also prohibits any false representation intended to mislead the patient, such as: distorting documents in such a way as to make the reader believe they are legal documents; falsifying the collector's identity; misstating the nature or status of a debt; or any other misleading designations.

Other prohibited practices include: depositing a post-dated check; causing collect charges on a telephone bill, telegram expenses, or other costs to be made to the consumer; or using a postcard to communicate with a consumer. Collectors should not leave messages on answering machines revealing that they're calling about a bill. This could be overheard by a third party.

Contacting the Patient by Mail

Within five days after the initial communication, the collector is obligated to send the patient written verification of the amount of the debt, and the creditor to whom the debt is owed. If the patient makes a written request for information or disputes any portion of the debt within 30 days, the collector must cease collection of the debt, or any disputed portion thereof.

If mailings are used to verify a patient's location, any language or symbol indicating that the communication relates to debt collection should be omitted from the stationery and envelope. Using a postcard to correct location information is also prohibited.

Locating the Patient

The collector is prohibited by law from communicating with a third party more than once, unless expressly requested to do so by that party, or if the collector believes the first response was erroneous or incomplete.

Once the collector knows the consumer is represented by an attorney, with respect to the debt, and knows the name and address of the attorney, the collector must not communicate with anyone else, unless the attorney fails to respond within a reasonable period of time. The law does not provide specific parameters for "a reasonable period of time." For your protection in lawsuits, it's a good idea to establish a written policy for your office that can be used as a defense.

Cutting Off Communication

Once patients notify the collector in writing that they refuse to pay the debt and want communications stopped, the collector cannot pursue further communications. The only communication allowed by the collector is to advise the consumer that efforts are being terminated, or to notify the consumer that legal action may or will be taken.

Enforcement

The FDCPA is enforced by the Federal Trade Commission. It can treat a violation of the Act as an unfair or deceptive practice under the law. Violators are also subject to civil penalties in federal and state courts.

EXCERPTS FROM THE FAIR DEBT COLLECTION PRACTICES ACT

TITLE 15. COMMERCE AND TRADE
CHAPTER 41 — CONSUMER CREDIT PROTECTION
SUBCHAPTER V — DEBT COLLECTION PRACTICES
Current through P.L. 104-333, approved 11-12-96

§ 1692a. Definitions

As used in this subchapter —

(1) The term "Commission" means the Federal Trade Commission.

(2) The term "communication" means the conveying of information regarding a debt directly or indirectly to any person through any medium.

(3) The term "consumer" means any natural person obligated or allegedly obligated to pay any debt.

(4) The term "creditor" means any person who offers or extends credit creating a debt or to whom a debt is owed, but such term does not include any person to the extent that he receives an assignment or transfer of a debt in default solely for the purpose of facilitating collection of such debt for another.

(5) The term "debt" means any obligation or alleged obligation of a consumer to pay money arising out of a transaction in which the money, property, insurance, or services which are the subject of the transaction are primarily for personal, family, or household purposes, whether or not such obligation has been reduced to judgment.

(6) The term "debt collector" means any person who uses any instrumentality of interstate commerce or the mails in any business the principal purpose of which is the collection of any debts, or who regularly collects or attempts to collect, directly or indirectly, debts owed or due or asserted to be owed or due another. Notwithstanding the exclusion provided by clause (F) of the last sentence of

continues

Excerpts continued

this paragraph, the term includes any creditor who, in the process of collecting his own debts, uses any name other than his own which would indicate that a third person is collecting or attempting to collect such debts. For the purpose of section 1692f(6) of this title, such term also includes any person who uses any instrumentality of interstate commerce or the mails in any business the principal purpose of which is the enforcement of security interests. The term does not include —

(A) Any officer or employee of a creditor while, in the name of the creditor, collecting debts for such creditor;

(B) Any person while acting as a debt collector for another person, both of whom are related by common ownership or affiliated by corporate control, if the person acting as a debt collector does so only for persons to whom it is so related or affiliated and if the principal business of such person is not the collection of debts;

(C) Any officer or employee of the United States or any State to the extent that collecting or attempting to collect any debt is in the performance of his official duties;

(D) Any person while serving or attempting to serve legal process on any other person in connection with the judicial enforcement of any debt;

(E) Any nonprofit organization which, at the request of consumers, performs bona fide consumer credit counseling and assists consumers in the liquidation of their debts by receiving payments from such consumers and distributing such amounts to creditor; and

(F) Any person collecting or attempting to collect any debt owed or due or asserted to be owed or due another to the extent such activity (i) is incidental to a bona fide fiduciary obligation or a bona fide escrow arrangement; (ii) concerns a debt which was originated by such person; (iii) concerns a debt which was not in default at the time it was obtained by such person; or (iv) concerns a debt obtained by such person as a secured party in a commercial credit transaction involving the creditor.

continues

Excerpts continued

(G) Redesignated.

(7) The term "location information" means a consumer's place of abode and his telephone number at such place, or his place of employment.

(8) The term "State" means any State, territory, or possession of the United States, the District of Columbia, the Commonwealth of Puerto Rico, or any political subdivision of any of the foregoing.

§ 1692b. Acquisition of Location Information

Any debt collector communicating with any person other than the consumer for the purpose of acquiring location information about the consumer shall -

(1) Identify himself, state that he is confirming or correcting location information concerning the consumer, and, only if expressly requested, identify his employer;

(2) Not state that such consumer owes any debt;

(3) Not communicate with any such person more than once unless requested to do so by such person or unless the debt collector reasonably believes that the earlier response of such person is erroneous or incomplete and that such person now has correct or complete location information;

(4) Not communicate by post card;

(5) Not use any language or symbol on any envelope or in the contents of any communication effected by the mails or telegram that indicates that the debt collector is in the debt collection business or that the communication relates to the collection of a debt; and

(6) After the debt collector knows the consumer is represented by an attorney with regard to the subject debt and has knowledge of, or can readily ascertain, such attorney's name and address, not communicate with any person other than that attorney, unless the attorney fails to respond within a reasonable period of time to communication from the debt collector.

continues

Excerpts continued

§ 1692c. Communication in Connection with Debt Collection

(a) Communication with Consumer Generally

Without the prior consent of the consumer given directly to the debt collector or the express permission of a court of competent jurisdiction, a debt collector may not communicate with a consumer in connection with the collection of any debt -

(1) At any unusual time or place or a time or place known or which should be known to be inconvenient to the consumer. In the absence of knowledge of circumstances to the contrary, a debt collector shall assume that the convenient time for communicating with a consumer is after 8 o'clock antemeridian and before 9 o'clock postmeridian, local time at the consumer's location;

(2) If the debt collector knows the consumer is represented by an attorney with respect to such debt and has knowledge of, or can readily ascertain, such attorney's name and address, unless the attorney fails to respond within a reasonable period of time to a communication from the debt collector or unless the attorney consents to direct communication with the consumer; or

(3) At the consumer's place of employment if the debt collector knows or has reason to know that the consumer's employer prohibits the consumer from receiving such communication.

(b) Communication with Third Parties

Except as provided in section 1692b of this title, without the prior consent of the consumer given directly to the debt collector, or the express permission of a court of competent jurisdiction, or as reasonably necessary to effectuate a post-judgment judicial remedy, a debt collector may not communicate, in connection with the collection of any debt, with any person other than the consumer, his attorney, a consumer reporting agency if otherwise permitted by law, the creditor, the attorney of the creditor, or the attorney of the debt collector.

(c) Ceasing Communication

continues

Excerpts continued

If a consumer notifies a debt collector in writing that the consumer refuses to pay a debt or that the consumer wishes the debt collector to cease further communication with the consumer, the debt collector shall not communicate further with the consumer with respect to such debt, except -

(1) To advise the consumer that the debt collector's further efforts are being terminated;

(2) To notify the consumer that the debt collector or creditor may invoke specified remedies which are ordinarily invoked by such debt collector or creditor; or

(3) Where applicable, to notify the consumer that the debt collector or creditor intends to invoke a specified remedy.

If such notice from the consumer is made by mail, notification shall be complete upon receipt.

(d) "Consumer" Defined

For the purpose of this section, the term "consumer" includes the consumer's spouse, parent (if the consumer is a minor), guardian, executor, or administrator.

§ 1692d. Harassment or Abuse

A debt collector may not engage in any conduct the natural consequence of which is to harass, oppress, or abuse any person in connection with the collection of a debt. Without limiting the general application of the foregoing, the following conduct is a violation of this section:

(1) The use or threat of use of violence or other criminal means to harm the physical person, reputation, or property of any person.

(2) The use of obscene or profane language or language the natural consequence of which is to abuse the hearer or reader.

(3) The publication of a list of consumers who allegedly refuse to pay debts, except to a consumer reporting agency or to persons meeting the requirements of section 1681a(f) or 1681b(3) of this title.

continues

Excerpts continued

(4) The advertisement for sale of any debt to coerce payment of the debt.

(5) Causing a telephone to ring or engaging any person in telephone conversation repeatedly or continuously with intent to annoy, abuse, or harass any person at the called number.

(6) Except as provided in section 1692b of this title, the placement of telephone calls without meaningful disclosure of the caller's identity.

§ 1692e. False or Misleading Representations

A debt collector may not use any false, deceptive, or misleading representation or means in connection with the collection of any debt. Without limiting the general application of the foregoing, the following conduct is a violation of this section:

(1) The false representation or implication that the debt collector is vouched for, bonded by, or affiliated with the United States or any State, including the use of any badge, uniform, or facsimile thereof.

(2) The false representation of -

(A) The character, amount, or legal status of any debt; or

(B) Any services rendered or compensation which may be lawfully received by any debt collector for the collection of a debt.

(3) The false representation or implication that any individual is an attorney or that any communication is from an attorney.

(4) The representation or implication that nonpayment of any debt will result in the arrest or imprisonment of any person or the seizure, garnishment, attachment, or sale of any property or wages of any person unless such action is lawful and the debt collector or creditor intends to take such action.

(5) The threat to take any action that cannot legally be taken or that is not intended to be taken.

(6) The false representation or implication that a sale, referral, or

continues

Excerpts continued

other transfer of any interest in a debt shall cause the consumer to -
    (A) Lose any claim or defense to payment of the debt; or
    (B) Become subject to any practice prohibited by this subchapter.
(7) The false representation or implication that the consumer committed any crime or other conduct in order to disgrace the consumer.
(8) Communicating or threatening to communicate to any person credit information which is known or which should be known to be false, including the failure to communicate that a disputed debt is disputed.
(9) The use or distribution of any written communication which simulates or is falsely represented to be a document authorized, issued, or approved by any court, official, or agency of the United States or any State, or which creates a false impression as to its source, authorization, or approval.
(10) The use of any false representation or deceptive means to collect or attempt to collect any debt or to obtain information concerning a consumer.
(11) The failure to disclose in the initial written communication with the consumer and, in addition, if the initial communication with the consumer is oral, in that initial oral communication, that the debt collector is attempting to collect a debt and that any information obtained will be used for that purpose, and the failure to disclose in subsequent communications that the communication is from a debt collector, except that this paragraph shall not apply to a formal pleading made in connection with a legal action.
(12) The false representation or implication that accounts have been turned over to innocent purchasers for value.
(13) The false representation or implication that documents are legal process.
(14) The use of any business, company, or organization name other than the true name of the debt collector's business, company, or organization.

continues

Excerpts continued

(15) The false representation or implication that documents are not legal process forms or do not require action by the consumer.

(16) The false representation or implication that a debt collector operates or is employed by a consumer reporting agency as defined by section 1681a(f) of this title.

§ 1692f. Unfair Practices

A debt collector may not use unfair or unconscionable means to collect or attempt to collect any debt. Without limiting the general application of the foregoing, the following conduct is a violation of this section:

(1) The collection of any amount (including any interest, fee, charge, or expense incidental to the principal obligation) unless such amount is expressly authorized by the agreement creating the debt or permitted by law.

(2) The acceptance by a debt collector from any person of a check or other payment instrument postdated by more than five days unless such person is notified in writing of the debt collector's intent to deposit such check or instrument not more than ten nor less than three business days prior to such deposit.

(3) The solicitation by a debt collector of any postdated check or other postdated payment instrument for the purpose of threatening or instituting criminal prosecution.

(4) Depositing or threatening to deposit any postdated check or other postdated payment instrument prior to the date on such check or instrument.

(5) Causing charges to be made to any person for communications by concealment of the true purpose of the communication. Such charges include, but are not limited to, collect telephone calls and telegram fees.

(6) Taking or threatening to take any nonjudicial action to effect dispossession or disablement of property if -

continues

Excerpts continued

(A) There is no present right to possession of the property claimed as collateral through an enforceable security interest;

(B) There is no present intention to take possession of the property; or

(C) The property is exempt by law from such dispossession or disablement.

(7) Communicating with a consumer regarding a debt by post card.

(8) Using any language or symbol, other than the debt collector's address, on any envelope when communicating with a consumer by use of the mails or by telegram, except that a debt collector may use his business name if such name does not indicate that he is in the debt collection business.

§ 1692g. Validation of Debts

(a) Notice of Debt; Contents

Within five days after the initial communication with a consumer in connection with the collection of any debt, a debt collector shall, unless the following information is contained in the initial communication or the consumer has paid the debt, send the consumer a written notice containing -

(1) The amount of the debt;

(2) The name of the creditor to whom the debt is owed;

(3) A statement that unless the consumer, within thirty days after receipt of the notice, disputes the validity of the debt, or any portion thereof, the debt will be assumed to be valid by the debt collector;

(4) A statement that if the consumer notifies the debt collector in writing within the thirty-day period that the debt, or any portion thereof, is disputed, the debt collector will obtain verification of the debt or a copy of a judgment against the consumer and a copy of such verification or judgment will be mailed to the consumer by the debt collector; and

continues

Excerpts continued

(5) A statement that, upon the consumer's written request within the thirty-day period, the debt collector will provide the consumer with the name and address of the original creditor, if different from the current creditor.

(b) Disputed Debts

If the consumer notifies the debt collector in writing within the thirty-day period described in subsection (a) of this section that the debt, or any portion thereof, is disputed, or that the consumer requests the name and address of the original creditor, the debt collector shall cease collection of the debt, or any disputed portion thereof, until the debt collector obtains verification of the debt or a copy of a judgment, or the name and address of the original creditor, and a copy of such verification or judgment, or name and address of the original creditor, is mailed to the consumer by the debt collector.

(c) Admission of Liability

The failure of a consumer to dispute the validity of a debt under this section may not be construed by any court as an admission of liability by the consumer.

§ 1692j. Furnishing Certain Deceptive Forms

(a) It is unlawful to design, compile, and furnish any form knowing that such form would be used to create the false belief in a consumer that a person other than the creditor of such consumer is participating in the collection of or in an attempt to collect a debt such consumer allegedly owes such creditor, when in fact such person is not so participating.

(b) Any person who violates this section shall be liable to the same extent and in the same manner as a debt collector is liable under section 1692k of this title for failure to comply with a provision of this subchapter.

continues

Excerpts continued

§ 1692k. Civil Liability

(a) Amount of Damages

Except as otherwise provided by this section, any debt collector who fails to comply with any provision of this subchapter with respect to any person is liable to such person in an amount equal to the sum of -

(1) Any actual damage sustained by such person as a result of such

failure;

(2)(A) In the case of any action by an individual, such additional damages as the court may allow, but not exceeding $1,000; or (B) In the case of a class action, (i) such amount for each named plaintiff as could be recovered under subparagraph (A), and (ii) such amount as the court may allow for all other class members, without regard to a minimum individual recovery, not to exceed the lesser of $500,000 or 1 percent of the net worth of the debt collector; and

(3) In the case of any successful action to enforce the foregoing liability, the costs of the action, together with a reasonable attorney's fee as determined by the court. On a finding by the court that an action under this section was brought in bad faith and for the purpose of harassment, the court may award to the defendant attorney's fees reasonable in relation to the work expended and costs.

(b) Factors Considered by Court

In determining the amount of liability in any action under subsection (a) of this section, the court shall consider, among other relevant factors -

(1) In any individual action under subsection (a)(2)(A) of this section, the frequency and persistence of noncompliance by the debt collector, the nature of such noncompliance, and the extent to which such noncompliance was intentional; or

(2) In any class action under subsection (a)(2)(B) of this section, the frequency and persistence of noncompliance by the debt collector, the nature of such noncompliance, the resources of the debt

continues

Excerpts continued

collector, the number of persons adversely affected, and the extent to which the debt collector's noncompliance was intentional.

(c) Intent

A debt collector may not be held liable in any action brought under this subchapter if the debt collector shows by a preponderance of evidence that the violation was not intentional and resulted from a bona fide error notwithstanding the maintenance of procedures reasonably adapted to avoid any such error.

(d) Jurisdiction

An action to enforce any liability created by this subchapter may be brought in any appropriate United States district court without regard to the amount in controversy, or in any other court of competent jurisdiction, within one year from the date on which the violation occurs.

(e) Advisory Opinions of Commission

No provision of this section imposing any liability shall apply to any act done or omitted in good faith in conformity with any advisory opinion of the Commission, notwithstanding that after such act or omission has occurred, such opinion is amended, rescinded, or determined by judicial or other authority to be invalid for any reason.

§ 1692l. Administrative Enforcement

(a) Federal Trade Commission

Compliance with this subchapter shall be enforced by the Commission, except to the extent that enforcement of the requirements imposed under this subchapter is specifically committed to another agency under subsection (b) of this section. For purpose of the exercise by the Commission of its functions and powers under the Federal Trade Commission Act, a violation of this subchapter shall be deemed an unfair or deceptive act or practice in violation of that Act. All of the functions and powers of the Commission under the Federal Trade Commission Act are available to the Commission to

continues

Excerpts continued

enforce compliance by any person with this subchapter, irrespective of whether that person is engaged in commerce or meets any other jurisdictional tests in the Federal Trade Commission Act, including the power to enforce the provisions of this subchapter in the same manner as if the violation had been a violation of a Federal Trade Commission trade regulation rule.

(b) Applicable Provisions of Law

Compliance with any requirements imposed under this subchapter shall be enforced under -

(1) Section 8 of the Federal Deposit Insurance Act [12 U.S.C.A. § 1818], in the case of -

(A) National banks, and Federal branches and Federal agencies of foreign banks, by the Office of the Comptroller of the Currency; (B) member banks of the Federal Reserve System (other than national banks), branches and agencies of foreign banks (other than Federal branches, Federal agencies, and insured State branches of foreign banks), commercial lending companies owned or controlled by foreign banks, and organizations operating under section 25 or 25(a) of the Federal Reserve Act [12 U.S.C.A. §§ 601 et seq., 611 et seq.], by the Board of Governors of the Federal Reserve System; and (C) banks insured by the Federal Deposit Insurance Corporation (other than members of the Federal Reserve System) and insured State branches of foreign banks, by the Board of Directors of the Federal Deposit Insurance Corporation;

(2) Section 8 of the Federal Deposit Insurance Act [12 U.S.C.A. § 1818], by the Director of the Office of Thrift Supervision, in the case of a savings association the deposits of which are insured by the Federal Deposit Insurance Corporation;

(3) The Federal Credit Union Act, by the National Credit Union Administration Board with respect to any Federal credit union;

(4) Subtitle IV of Title 49, by the Secretary of Transportation, with respect to all carriers subject to the jurisdiction of the Surface Transportation Board;

continues

Excerpts continued

(5) The Federal Aviation Act of 1958, by the Secretary of Transportation with respect to any air carrier or any foreign air carrier subject to that Act; and

(6) The Packers and Stockyards Act, 1921 (except as provided in section 406 of that Act), by the Secretary of Agriculture with respect to any activities subject to that Act.

The terms used in paragraph (1) that are not defined in this subchapter or otherwise defined in section 3(s) of the Federal Deposit Insurance Act (12 U.S.C. 1813(s)) shall have the meaning given to them in section 1(b) of the International Banking Act of 1978 (12 U.S.C. 3101).

(c) Agency Powers

For the purpose of the exercise by any agency referred to in subsection (b) of this section of its powers under any Act referred to in that subsection, a violation of any requirement imposed under this subchapter shall be deemed to be a violation of a requirement imposed under that Act. In addition to its powers under any provision of law specifically referred to in subsection (b) of this section, each of the agencies referred to in that subsection may exercise, for the purpose of enforcing compliance with any requirement imposed under this subchapter any other authority conferred on it by law, except as provided in subsection (d) of this section.

(d) Rules and Regulations

Neither the Commission nor any other agency referred to in subsection (b) of this section may promulgate trade regulation rules or other regulations with respect to the collection of debts by debt collectors as defined in this subchapter.

§ 1692n. Relation to State Laws

This subchapter does not annul, alter, affect, or exempt any person subject to the provisions of this subchapter from complying with the laws of any State with respect to debt collection practices,

continues

Excerpts continued

except to the extent that those laws are inconsistent with any provision of this subchapter, and then only to the extent of the inconsistency. For purposes of this section, a State law is not inconsistent with this subchapter if the protection such law affords any consumer is greater than the protection provided by this subchapter.

§ 1692o. Exemption for State Regulation

The Commission shall by regulation exempt from the requirements of this subchapter any class of debt collection practices within any State if the Commission determines that under the law of that State that class of debt collection practices is subject to requirements substantially similar to those imposed by this subchapter, and that there is adequate provision for enforcement.

APPENDIX A

Collector Resources

Health care collectors face myriad challenges in collecting accounts, and there are multiple sources that can help in that endeavor. Professional associations are an excellent starting point to gain access to professional contacts, educational materials, workshops, and conferences.

In addition, outsourcing outstanding receivables is a viable option to be tapped based on established policies. The decision of when to outsource outstanding receivables will vary by facility and staffing size. For instance, some facilities opt to outsource small patient-pay balances immediately while retaining in house large-dollar third-party-payer accounts as the primary focus for staff employees. Other facilities may outsource collections of accounts based on age, or if a clean up is required to regain internal control of accounts receivable management.

Among the most necessary and effective tools for health care collectors are software systems that provide automated work queues, tracking, and documentation of collection follow-up activity. With that in mind, several vendors are included among the listed resources.

The high degree of regulation and compliance issues makes it imperative that health care collectors avail themselves of federal regulatory agencies and accreditation agencies to gain insights into effective practices and compliance issues.

The resources included here, beginning with professional associations and including outsourcing firms that specialize in accounts receivable management, are provided as a starting point.

Through these suggested resources, you will find colleagues within the American Collectors Association. In addition, you can consider firms with services and systems that can enhance collections operations within your organization, such as Managed Healthcare Information Services, a firm that seeks to provide the most extensive and most current insurance master file data to improve health care provider organizations' billing and collections efforts.

It must be emphasized that the following contacts are resources to help guide you as you launch a diligent search to gather information and investigate resources to improve the effectiveness of collections in your organization. The fact that an organization is listed should not be construed as an endorsement of the organization.

PROFESSIONAL ASSOCIATIONS

American Association of Healthcare Administrative Management
1200 19th Street, NW
Suite 300
Washington, DC 20036
202/857-1179
www.aaham.org

American Collectors Association
4040 West 70th Street
P.O. Box 39106
Minneapolis, MN 55439
612/928-8000
www.collector.com

American College of Healthcare Executives
One North Franklin Street
Suite 1700
Chicago, IL 60606-3491
312/424-2800
www.ache.org

American Health Information Management Association
919 North Michigan Avenue
Suite 1400
Chicago, IL 60611
312/787-2672
www.ahima.org

American Health Lawyers Association
1120 Connecticut Avenue, NW
Suite 950
Washington, DC 20036
202/833-1100
www.healthlawyers.org

American Hospital Association
One North Franklin
Chicago, IL 60606
312/422-2000
www.aha.org

American Medical Association
515 North State Street
Chicago, IL 60610
312/464-5000
www.ama-assn.org

Healthcare Financial Management Association
2 Westbrook Corporate Center
Suite 700
Westchester, IL 60154
800/252-HFMA (4362)
www.hfma.org

Health Information Management Systems Society (HIMSS)
230 East Ohio Street
Suite 500
Chicago, IL 60611-3269
312/664-4467
www.himss.org

Joint Commission on Accreditation of Healthcare Organizations
919 North Michigan Avenue
Suite 1400
Chicago, IL 60611
312/787-2672
www.jcaho.org

Medical Group Management Association
104 Inverness Terrace East
Englewood, CO 80112-5306
303/799-1111
877/275-6462
www.mgma.com

GOVERNMENT AGENCIES VIA THE WEB

Office of Inspector General (OIG)
www.dhhs.gov/oig

Health Care Financing Administration
www.hcfa.gov

Federal Register
www.access.gpo.gov/su_docs/aces/aces140.html

Department of Health and Human Services
www.dhhs.gov

Home page for any state in the United States
www.state.[state postal abbreviation].us
   State pages provide access to state-specific information on insurance commissioner's office, workers' compensation, and other issues that will vary by state.

TRICARE support office
www.tso.osd.mil

SYSTEM VENDORS AND OUTSOURCING AND ACCOUNTS RECEIVABLE MANAGEMENT FIRMS

Corus Bank
Corus Medical Finance Program
P.O. Box 7966
Chicago, IL 60680
800/544-5647
www.corusbank.com
   The medical finance program works with health care provider organizations to maximize self-pay receivables performance.

EDI-USA
1 Landmark Square
Suite 300
Stamford, CT 06901
203/978-2929
www.ediusa.com

Nationwide electronic network privately owned by 13 Blue Cross and Blue Shield plans. Services include electronic claims submission, remittance advice, funds transfer, and interactive eligibility information.

Healthcare Data Exchange Corp. (HDX)
300 Lindenwood Drive
Suite 200
Malvern, PA 19355
610/219-1600
www.hdx.com

Company that provides integrated health care electronic data interchange (EDI) network services, including eligibility, verification, claims, and remittance services.

HSS Inc.
2321 Whitney Avenue
4th Floor
Hamden, CT 06518
800/999-3747
www.HSSWeb.com

Software company specializing in coding, reimbursement, and profiling of health care issues. HSS seeks to assist the health care industry in understanding and improving technologies for management finance and delivery of medical care.

IDX Systems Corp.
1400 Shelbourne Road
P.O. Box 1070
Burlington, VT 05402-1070
802/862-1022
www.idx.com

Health care information solutions firm serving provider organizations from physician offices to integrated delivery networks.

Information Resource Products Inc.
5 Alexander Road
Billerica, MA 01821-5032
800/634-0496
www.irp.com

Develops software tools for the health care industry. Specializes in encoding and grouping software to classify cases and medical records for payment and case-mix measurement.

Managed Healthcare Information Services
658 Commerce Drive
Suite D
Roseville, CA 95678
916/784-6800
www.payerID.com

Serves as a data warehouse for health plan and workers' compensation payers so that health care provider organizations can maintain current insurance master file information.

NDC Health Information Services (National Data Corporation)
1 National Data Plaza
Atlanta, GA 30329-2010
800/778-6711
www.ndchealth.com

Provides EDI transaction capabilities, software solutions, and business office services to health care provider organizations.

National Healthcare Review Inc.
22120 Clarendon Street
Suite 300
Woodland Hills, CA 91367
800/423-3097
www.nhri.com
   A clinical-financial management services firm that specializes in clinical auditing and coding.

Outsource Inc.
N27 W23713 Paul Road
Unit E
Pewaukee, WI 53072
800/799-7469
e-mail: outsourc@execpc.com
   Specializes in accounts receivable management, with special focus on billing and self-pay accounts management.

Quantum Collections
3224 Civic Center Drive
North Las Vegas, NV 89030
702/633-8000
   National organization providing complete collection services.

Appendix B

Common Legal Questions

Q What makes contacting a debtor illegal? Is a collector allowed to send a postcard to a debtor asking the debtor to call the collector? Also, is a collector allowed to make collect phone calls to a debtor regarding a debt collection matter?

A Under the Fair Debt Collection Practices Act (FDCPA), both of these actions are illegal. However, the FDCPA applies to third-party collectors only. To be safe, before original creditors use either of the above communication tactics, they should check their state laws. Many states adopt their own version of the FDCPA, and some have even more stringent rules that could make such contact methods illegal.

Under section 808 of the FDCPA, points five and eight specifically prohibit contacting debtors through the use of collect telephone calls and postcards. These points also prohibit collect telegram fees and any other method of communication that would cause charges to be made to any person through that communication.

These methods of communication are prohibited to protect the debtor. The very nature of a postcard allows it to be read by anyone who handles it. This could be damaging to the reputation, employment, or general well-being of a debtor, and under current interpretation of the FDCPA, the responsibility for the consequences lies solely with the collector who sent the card.

Collect phone calls and collect telegrams are prohibited as they are considered a form of harassment. The rule also mentions any means of communication that would bring charges to the debtor through a concealment of the true nature of the communication.

Q Are spouses legally responsible for each other's medical debts, regardless of whether they have signed an agreement?

A The answer to this question depends on the particular laws of each state in which the medical services were provided.

Many states follow the doctrine of necessities, which initially required only the husband to be responsible for necessary goods and services provided to the wife. Some states have expanded the doctrine of necessities to make it reciprocal between husbands and wives. Other states have statutes that set out the liability of spouses for the other's necessary goods and services.

The doctrine of necessities is a common law that recognizes the special relationship between spouses. It is also an attempt to provide special protection to women, who, at the time the doctrine was formulated, were in many cases unable to hold property in their own name. Any property owned by a woman at the time of marriage automatically became the property of her husband. Courts therefore found an obligation on the part of husbands to pay for goods and services, such as food, clothing, shelter, and medical care provided to their wives.

Legislatures expanded on the court-made law in some states and recognized the obligations that arise from the special relationship between spouses. In today's society, it only makes sense that spouses are financially responsible for the important things in life, with medical care certainly at the top of the list. It is the same kind of special relationship that creates the obligation of parents to pay for the medical and other necessary services provided to their children.

Q What should I do when a patient declares bankruptcy?

A The first thing to do is STOP EVERYTHING! Don't make collection calls. Don't send any collection letters. The filing of bankruptcy triggers what is know as the "automatic stay." This means all actions by creditors must stop unless the bankruptcy court decides otherwise.

The next step for collectors is to determine what type of bankruptcy the debtor has filed. There are two types: Chapter 7 and Chapter 13.

Chapter 7 bankruptcy: This will usually eliminate all of the debtor's outstanding legal obligation for unsecured debt. An unsecured debt isn't backed by any form of collateral. Most medical bills in this situation will be unsecured debt. If a medical bill is considered a secured debt, consult your attorney about collection procedures.

More often than not, there is no payment to unsecured creditors under Chapter 7 bankruptcy. In most jurisdictions, the bankruptcy notice tells the creditor not to file a claim unless notified to do so by the court. If you are advised to file a claim, do so immediately. The notice to file a claim means there are some assets left over for general, unsecured creditors. The only way a creditor can share in the assets is by filing a claim.

Chapter 13 bankruptcy: In this type of bankruptcy, there is almost always some payment of general, unsecured creditors. The way to participate is, again, to file a claim.

The bankruptcy court will advise creditors of the last date a claim can be filed. In the event the creditor is aware of the bankruptcy filing, but hasn't received official notice, the creditor must still take steps to file a claim. If this isn't done, the creditor runs the risk of not receiving payment.

After filing the claim, try to find out when the plan for payment of claims was approved by the court. Once the plan is approved, the debtor is required to make payment to a trustee. The trustee then disburses the funds — first to secured creditors, then to unsecured creditors.

Creditors should contact the trustee from time to time to check the status of the claim and the payments they should expect. Most Chapter 13 trustees are very cooperative and will advise creditors of the claim status when asked.

Q: Is it ever acceptable to retain overpayment?

A: The law pertaining to the retention or restitution of overpayments is governed by equitable principles, which means the outcome of each case is governed by the applicable facts. Therefore, one can only discuss general legal principles that have been traditionally applied to overpayments.

Typically, an overpayment happens when an insurer mistakenly overpays a patient or provider. Such overpayments are usually the result of a mistake surrounding the claim or a mistake of law regarding the insurer's contractual obligation to pay. This distinction isn't always clear and must be determined on a case-by-case basis.

A mistake of law occurs if the insurer makes a payment or overpayment under a policy based on a misinterpretation of the policy's language or coverage limits. When this happens, the insurer is only eligible for restitution if there's evidence of:

- fraud on the part of the payee
- duress
- improper conduct by the payee
- unjust enrichment of the insured (the insured was paid twice)

Examples pertaining to mistakes of fact are payments made by the insurer due to administrative error or a misunderstanding of the facts surrounding a claim. In these cases, the insurer may generally recover such payment, unless the insured is in a position wherein it would be unjust to require a refund.

However, the general rule as to recovery of payment has not been held to apply when an innocent third-party creditor, such as a health care provider, is involved, unless the third-party creditor caused the overpayment by submitting a claim with errors. This exception was clearly put forth in the case *Federated Mutual Insurance Co. v. Good Samaritan Hospital.*

In this case, the plaintiff insurer mistakenly overpaid Good Samaritan Hospital by more than $7,700. The hospital returned more than $5,800 to the insurance company, but it kept almost $2,200 of the overpayment, which it applied to the insured's hospital bill. Federated Insurance subsequently brought an action to recover this overpayment. Because the overpayment was made solely due to the insurance company's own mistake and lack of care, the court held that the hospital wasn't required to return the overpayment. The court cited the following reasons to justify the ruling:

To subject a hospital to possible refund liability if the insurer later discovers a mistake in overpayment, lasting until all such claims were barred by the statutes of limitations, would be to place an undue burden of contingent liability on such institutions. Hospitals would be safe only by requiring insurers to pay benefits directly to the insured patient, and then by accepting payment directly from the patient. By this ruling, we place the burden for determining the limits of policy liability squarely upon the only party in a position to know the policy provisions and its liability under the contract of insurance. Someone must suffer the loss, and as between plaintiff insurer and defendant hospital, the party making the mistake should bear that loss.

Important: The ruling for this case applies only when a third-party creditor is involved. Although Federated Insurance didn't have a right of restitution against the hospital, it would have had a right of restitution against the insured patient unless the patient could demonstrate that he or she relied on the overpayment and would be harmed by repaying it.

Q What makes a payment acceptable? If a patient makes very small monthly payments, which are accepted by the provider, is the provider legally bound to continue accepting payments of that size? And is the provider prevented from taking any additional action after having accepted small payments for a period of time?

A The laws vary from state to state, but in general, for parties to be bound to an agreement, there must be three essential elements: offer, acceptance, and consideration. The original agreement to provide medical services in return for payment constitutes the offer and acceptance. The consideration is the actual provision of medical services and the benefit that flows to the patient. Once health care services have been performed, the provider is entitled to payment. That means payment in full as soon as the services have been provided.

As a practical matter, with health insurers paying a substantial part of the cost of health care, most providers are willing to wait for payment from the insurance company. In the event the whole bill isn't paid by insurance, providers are often willing to accept monthly payments from the patient. The fact that the provider doesn't demand immediate and full payment does *not* create a new binding agreement requiring the provider to continue to accept small payments. However, if a provider accepts small payments over a period of time, it could be constituted as an agreement to accept that amount, or a modification of an existing agreement.

Some people are under the impression that as long as they make any amount of payment, a creditor is required to accept that payment and not take any additional action to attempt to collect. This isn't entirely true. The creditor can take action, including sending the account to a collection agency or lawyer. But there may be an implied rescission of the original agreement. The consideration would then be an additional promise to perform on a broken agreement.

Because of this gray area, it's good policy to draw up an agreement accepting payments of a certain amount for one year, then re-evaluate the amount on a certain date. This agreement would be decided after proof of income and debt was given. With solid proof of an agreement between your hospital and the patient, there is little room for doubt or misunderstanding of how much is owed when, and what the consequences for small or late payments are.

Q What are the requirements for collecting during an insurance investigation?

A Put simply, if a provider has properly submitted a patient's claim for services to the insurer on behalf of the patient, the provider then has every right to begin collection efforts against the patient, as long as those efforts are in conformance with the Fair Debt Collection Practices Act (FDCPA).

Although each situation is unique and should be analyzed individually, most of the cases involve an insurer providing some type of medical insurance to an individual through a contract between the patient and the insurance company. The health care provider is not an immediate party to this contract. As a result, any and all problems regarding an insurer's paying the bills of a patient are ultimately between the patient and the insurance company.

The catch is, as a service, health care providers usually accept the responsibility of properly submitting claims to an insurance company on behalf of the patient after services have been provided. In accepting this duty, a provider must take all reasonable steps necessary to perform it. This includes submitting the patient's claim in conformance with that particular insurer's policies and procedures and within the insurer's deadlines.

If a provider improperly submits a claim to an insurance company or doesn't provide the requisite information to the insurer, the provider may have breached the duty of properly submitting the patient's claims. In this situation, aggressively pursuing a patient for collection purposes would be imprudent and possibly in violation of the "good faith" requirements of the FDCPA. Therefore, it's necessary for a provider to ensure it has adequately performed its duties before aggressively pursuing collection from a patient.

Pending insurance claims are a common problem, particularly among long-term care facilities. For a typical example, assume a patient is admitted to a nursing home for skilled nursing care. The patient has Medicare coverage as well as a Medicare supplemental policy purchased from a private insurer, which covers the patient's medical expenses for skilled nursing care. Further assume that Medicare has already reimbursed the facility for the first 100 days of the patient's medical expenses related to skilled nursing care as defined in the Medicare rules. The supplemental policy will provide coverage for medical expenses related to skilled nursing care after the patient's first 100 days of Medicare have expired.

After day 101 of the patient's stay, the facility diligently performs its duty of submitting claims for payment to the patient's private insurer under the supplemental policy. Sixty days later, the insurance company responds with a denial, stating the care provided does not constitute skilled nursing care, a term the commercial policy defines more narrowly than Medicare does.

Important: If you receive any correspondence from the insurer indicating a possible denial or limitation of benefits, you should immediately notify the patient or the patient's legal representative and discuss alternative payment arrangements. By providing this prompt notification, you also ensure that the patient or the patient's legal representative can file a timely appeal with the insurer. You also ensure that the patient or legal representative can take any other legal action they deem appropriate.

Although the denial is unfortunate for the patient, the facility has no further obligation to the patient regarding the claims it has submitted, unless the insurer asks for more documentation from the facility to aid in its determination of whether skilled nursing care was provided. Therefore, a health care provider can pursue collection efforts against a patient and not violate the FDCPA, even though the patient has pending medical claims with an insurance company.

Q If a health insurance company issues a check to both the health care provider and the patient, and the patient endorses the check and is successful in cashing it without the endorsement of the health care provider, does the health care provider have recourse against anyone?

A Patients who engage in this kind of fraud, either by endorsing the name of the health care provider or by simply sneaking the check through with only one endorsement, are unlikely to repay the money they have come by. In the event the check is made only to the patient and the patient does not pay the money to the health care provider, the health care provider should immediately turn the account over for suit. It is important to pursue these cases as quickly as possible since the patient who keeps the insurance money is probably in a poor financial situation.

In the event two endorsements are required on the check, and the health care provider does not endorse the check, the first step is to advise the insurance company of the fraud. The company can then recover the money from whomever accepted the check without proper endorsement.

Suppose the patient takes the check made out to both the health care provider and the patient, and endorses only the patient's name, cashes the check, then dies. If the patient has an estate, the first thing for the health care provider to do is file a claim in the estate for the outstanding balance. The next step, whether the patient has an estate or not, is to notify the insurance company that the check was cashed without the proper endorsement. Then the insurance company can recover the funds from the entity that accepted the check from the patient.

It's a much quicker remedy to have the insurance company take action against the entity that accepted the check, rather than attempting to pursue that entity on behalf of the health care provider. The most important thing about pursuing this situation is that the action be taken quickly. It becomes much more difficult to pursue these matters as time passes.

Q Can a patient's request for a release of information be denied due to an outstanding bill?

A There may not be a federal regulation, but some states have case law ruling against such practices. What's more important is, by withholding a patient's information, you are affecting that patient's care. The information you have is important to the patient's new physician, and without it, the physician may overlook a part of the patient's treatment or even misdiagnose the patient's problem. This could result in a lawsuit against the new physician, which would be very difficult to defend against.

The patient may have an outstanding balance with you, but in the interest of the patient's care and in the spirit of fair business, releasing the patient's records is recommended.

Q As a collector, can I affect a debtor's credit rating?

A First and foremost, a creditor can only report truthful information, such as a debtor who did not pay a bill on time, to a credit reporting agency. If information is disputed, the furnisher of the information must notify the credit bureau of the dispute and investigate it. If a correction is required, the supplier of information must take reasonable steps to ensure that the incorrect information is removed and doesn't reappear.

Most credit reporting agencies require membership before they will accept information from a creditor. Membership is generally not very expensive, and usually entitles the members to receive credit reports that are not available to the general public. Members are typically charged a nominal fee for these reports. Trans Union, a national credit reporting agency, charges a standard membership fee of $10 per month, for example. (Note: This fee will vary depending on services required.)

If a hospital or doctor's office has a patient with an outstanding debt that it has tried to collect, it can note its collection efforts with the credit reporting agency. While this won't help collect the debt, it will smudge the debtor's credit rating.

Tip: It's always a good idea to notify the debtor that you plan on reporting the debt to a credit reporting agency. This might be all the incentive they need to clear up the debt.

A second method for impacting a debtor's credit rating is to file a lawsuit against the debtor and proceed to judgment. Most credit reporting agencies generally make civil judgments a part of a person's credit history. A properly perfected judgment in some states also becomes a lien against real estate owned by the debtor against which the judgment is entered. This entry of judgment can hinder or prevent the debtor from buying or selling real estate until the judgment has been resolved.

Finally, the most common way to affect a debtor's credit rating is to refer the account to a collection agency. Collection agencies, as a regular practice, report past-due accounts to the local credit reporting agency.

Q When can you sue for payment?

A For self-pay accounts, you can sue for payment under these four conditions: breach of contract; breach of implied contract; Quantum Meruit, which is an equity action; and the Necessaries Doctrine. Each of these conditions has its own qualifications as well.

Breach of contract requires a written or verbal agreement to pay for medical services. You can sue anyone who signs that agreement, so it's to your advantage to get as many people to sign as possible. You can also sue anyone who verbally agrees to pay, although that's harder than doing so with a written agreement.

Problems include:
- the language of the financial agreement. The language may have been confusing. If there wasn't a meeting of the minds, the defendant(s) can claim they didn't know they had to pay.
- whether the agreement was voluntary. The patient may have been unconscious, drunk, or otherwise experiencing impaired judgment when making payment arrangements.
- the amount owed for the treatment. Courts may not want to make someone pay. The court doesn't want to make someone a pauper. If that is the case, you would then absorb the expense.

With **breach of implied contract**, no express agreement was made to pay for services given. However, the premise is that the patient knew or should have known the provider expected to be paid for the services, and by accepting the services, the patient *implied agreement* to pay. The defense against this is to prove the patient was unclear on the agreement and whether the treatment was accepted. If the patient was unconscious or sedated, acceptance can be disputed.

Quantum Meruit is used when there is no express or implied agreement to pay for services. The action is based on the premise that receipt of medical services without payment is a windfall (unfair advantage), and that to maintain equity, the court should not allow retention of that windfall. Because you can't exactly take health care services back, you make the recipient pay.

The Necessaries Doctrine falls under state law, but does not apply in all states. Under the law in most states, a person is obligated to pay for medical services he or she receives. That person may also be obligated to pay for necessary medical services received by a spouse and/or a minor child.

Problems include the amount of payment (once again, not wanting to make anyone a pauper) and the necessity of the treatment. Under the Fair Debt Collection Practices Act, a patient can only be sued for the amount of money he or she agreed to pay.

Suing insurance carriers: Two conditions exist when an insurance carrier could be sued to obtain insurance benefits: claim for plan benefits/breach of contract, and claim for damages. Again, they have their own qualifications.

Claim for plan benefits is used when the claim is governed by ERISA or FEHBA, with breach of contract coming into play when the claim falls outside the scope of these federal laws. ERISA is the Employee Retirement Income Security Act. It mainly governs health insurance provided as a benefit of employment. FEHBA is the Federal Employee Health Benefits Act and governs all health insurance benefits provided as a benefit to federal employees.

These laws are especially significant because they're federal laws, thereby overruling most state laws that relate to insurance benefits, no matter what the state laws say.

You can sue on the basis of claim for plan benefits when the denial is on the basis of:

- medical necessity
- pre-existing condition
- usual and customary rates issues
- not a covered provider or facility
- services fall within an exclusion to coverage

The action can also be used in cases where the plan administrator failed to offer COBRA.

If the claim is not governed by ERISA or FEHBA, in addition to suing for breach of contract, it's possible to sue if the conduct of the payer constitutes a violation of state law relating to unfair insurance practices. That's the condition where you refer to state law. If federal law doesn't apply, state law takes over and you can sue on that basis.

Problems include exhaustion of administrative remedies. Under both ERISA and FEHBA, an insured is entitled to appeal a denied claim. In order to sue for payment, a timely request must be filed. For FEHBA, timely means within six months of the denial. With ERISA, the request must be filed within 60 days of the denial.

Defendants in an ERISA action would be the health plan, the plan administrator, and the claims administrator. In a FEHBA action, defendants would include the United States Office of Personnel Management.

These cases can be a bit strange or complicated because you're actually suing a health plan, not a person. That makes it difficult to attack errors made by the defendant.

Suing on the basis of claim for damages falls entirely under state law. In this case, you are suing an insurer because the patient had no plan benefits, but the insurer or plan administrator led you to believe there were benefits. This is most likely to occur with:

- the insurer's misquoting benefits during a verification of those benefits
- preauthorization of treatment, then a denial of payment due to lack of medical necessity

When claiming for damages, the health care provider is claiming the insurer is now refusing payment it said it would provide. You are now depending on the payment you were promised. The "damages" referred to is the amount of money you expected to receive based on the misrepresentation that was made.

Problems include:

- ERISA pre-emption. Because this is based on state law, the case would be invalid if overruled by federal law.
- documentation of the misrepresentation. Can you prove the benefits were ever quoted, or payment was promised?

Unlike other legal cases, attorney's fees are not typically worked into the award provided. In self-pay cases, these fees are only awarded if the financial agreement made with the patient specifies that the patient must pay the fees in the event of a default of the agreement. However, some states have statutes that allow for the collection of attorney's fees.

In cases of breach of contract, each party bears its own attorney's fees unless an agreement is made otherwise.

When suing for claims for plan benefits, attorney's fees can be awarded to the winning party at the discretion of the court. In cases involving ERISA, the courts have developed a test to decide if attorney's fees should be included as part of the decision. Items to be investigated include:

- the degree of the opponent's bad faith or culpability
- the opponent's ability to pay the fee

- whether awarding the attorney's fees will have a deterrent effect against future violations
- whether a significant legal issue was resolved
- how the parties' positions benefited ERISA issues
- if plan participants benefited from the actions
- any other relevant matters the court decides to consider

Once you've gotten to the point where you find you have grounds to sue and could benefit from doing so, you still have to find which court has jurisdiction and begin the proceedings. Jurisdiction determines which court you must go to with the lawsuit, and in some cases, it may prevent you from proceeding with the case.

Subject matter jurisdiction means the court has the power to hear the case. Federal courts have the power to hear cases that involve a federal question, such as claims for ERISA or FEHBA. Federal courts would also handle cases involving diversity of citizenship, which is a case where the parties are residents of different states and the damages exceed a minimum dollar threshold. If you don't meet or exceed that threshold, you can't proceed with the case in federal court.

State courts, on the other hand, have the power to hear cases that involve state law claims, including breach of contract and actions for damages. They also have concurrent jurisdiction for ERISA benefits claims.

Once jurisdiction has been determined, you must file a complaint, which includes a filing fee. This fee varies based on the state or court in which the case will be held. There are two requirements for filing the claim, aside from paying the fee:

1. All claims that arise from the same interaction or occurrence or series of occurrences must be brought in under the same lawsuit.
2. The lawsuit must be filed before the statute of limitations.

After the complaint is served, the defendant has between 20 and 30 days to respond. This response can be in the form of an answer or in the form of a Motion to Dismiss. This can be the most difficult time of all.

It may seem to take forever to go from the complaint stage to the trial. In the meantime, your opponent is trying to throw the trial out of court. While the defendant has a set time to respond, the court may not decide what to do for years. Most often, the court sits on the decision because the judges simply don't know what to do. They're not health care experts, and in many cases, both parties seem right. Typically, if you're suing a patient for payment, the case is more likely to be thrown out than if you're suing an insurer because sympathies frequently lie with the individual.

If the defendant files an answer, rather than an attempt to dismiss, or if a dismissal is denied, the defendant raises the defenses against the lawsuit and may file counterclaims or cross-claims, making the case even more complex.

Meanwhile, each party is entitled to discovery — the recovery of whatever information would help in the case. When this process is complete, another obstacle arises as either party can file a Motion for Summary Judgment.

A summary judgment means there is no genuine issue of material fact, and the question at hand is a question of law that the court should decide without a trial. This can be for a specific issue within the case or for the entire case.

After the waiting and the continual attempts at dismissal, your case may actually make it to trial. Basically, you either win or lose at the trial. If you win, an award will be given. If you lose, you have the right to appeal.

The burden of proof for an appeal is extremely high. You must demonstrate that there was a harmful error or that the trial court abused its discretion in the decision it made. And once again, there is a cost for filing.

Avoiding problems: As you can see, suing for payment is a grueling and often expensive process that should not be undertaken on a whim. If a patient or insurer owes you enough money to be worth the cost of going to court, or if you're having a lot of problems with an insurer, it may be worth your while to pursue the case. Because your actions will be attacked as much as the defendant's actions, observe the following guidelines:

1. Financial agreements
   - Have each patient or responsible party sign the agreement.
   - Make sure the signature is voluntary.

- Be sure the financial agreement allows you to collect attorney's fees and perhaps even interest in the event the responsible party breaches the agreement.
- Makes sure the language of other documents, such as the assignment of benefits, doesn't imply that the patient or responsible party will be responsible for less than full charges.

2. Assignment of benefits
   - Make sure your language allows you, the health care provider, the right to file appeals and lawsuits on behalf of the patient in the event of nonpayment.
3. Exhaustion of administrative remedies
   - Make every appeal you can.
   - File all appeals before the deadline expires.
4. Business records
   - Make sure your business records are understandable, legible, and complete. If they're not, it reflects badly on you and damages your standing in the case.
   - Make sure your witnesses print their names.
5. Language
   - Avoid using vague descriptions or confusing terms in your contracts and forms. Days or weeks may be spent in court going over your financial agreement to decide if it's confusing, what it's implying, and if a person could be reasonably expected to understand it.
   - In many cases, FEHBA will not accept contracts with confusing language, and you may lose a case on those grounds alone.
6. Grounds to sue
   - When suing, sue as many people on as many grounds as you can. This "shotgun method" gives your opponent more items to attack, but it increases your chances that one item will stick, and one is all you need.

Q Are letters of protection on auto accident claims designed to protect the hospital or the patient?

A The answer is, it depends on who drafts the letter of protection. An attorney has a duty to protect the interests of his or her client. Thus, if the attorney who drafts the letter of protection is not your attorney, you can bet your interests are not being fully protected.

The most common letters of protection are drafted by the patient's attorney and may not provide the kind of protection you would like your patients to receive. They are either very vague or they guarantee only that the hospital will be paid in full if a settlement is reached and the amount of the settlement is enough to pay all past bills and all future anticipated expenses.

In most cases, after the lawsuit is resolved, whether through settlement or judgment, the patient's attorney will attempt to negotiate payment of less than the full amount of the bill. The letter of protection provides little if any recourse, except to reject the offers and do your best to collect from the patient after the settlement proceeds have been disbursed.

In addition to obtaining a letter of protection, always file a lien and bill all insurers, including the auto insurance carrier and the health insurer. Be sure to bill the auto insurance carrier with your assignment of benefits so the carrier is on notice that you're entitled to receive payment directly.

Keep in mind, most health insurance plans have timely filing deadlines that do not take into account the period of time you have to wait until the auto claim is resolved. If the auto claim does not result in full payment to the hospital, and the hospital misses the health insurer's timely filing deadline, the only recourse for payment may be the patient. Thus, it's recommended that you bill the health insurer at the time services are rendered.

While you may have problems collecting from the health insurer until the auto claim is resolved, those health insurers that are obligated to pay immediately after personal injury protection benefits are exhausted will often pay you immediately, then exercise their right of subrogation against the patient.

Q **What is the statute of limitations on past-due accounts?**

A There is really no time limit for attempting to collect payment on a past-due medical bill. However, after the statute of limitations expires, it's unlikely that collection efforts will be successful since you have no recourse. Also, you may have difficulty retaining a collection agency or an attorney to pursue collection efforts on your behalf because at least one court has ruled that efforts by a debt collector to collect a debt after the expiration of the statute of limitations is a violation of the Fair Debt Collection Practices Act.

The statute of limitations refers to the time limit allowed by law for bringing a lawsuit. It varies both by state and by cause of action. Claims for several past-due medical bills may give rise to a number of different causes of action, and in most states, the statute of limitations is not the same for each claim.

Some states have very long statutes of limitations for the type of causes of action that arise from nonpayment of a medical bill, even as long as eight or 10 years. However, as a practical matter, if you do not make ongoing efforts to collect on a past-due account, even a lawsuit filed before the expiration of the statute of limitations may be unsuccessful because of the equitable defenses available to the creditor. Basically, these defenses allow a court to dismiss a case if you fail to take action to protect your right to payment, which is only fair considering health care providers sometimes make mistakes in connection with bills, and individuals don't tend to keep their medical records indefinitely. It would be inequitable to allow a provider to sit on its rights for eight to 10 years, then begin its efforts to collect from the patient at a point where the patient may not even remember receiving the services, or may not have the records necessary to evaluate whether the payment is owed.

The best practice is to make a concerted effort to collect on an account from the time services are rendered. If you are billing an insurer and you have the right to bill the patient in the event of nonpayment by the insurer, send the patient regular statements. Your statements should indicate that if the insurer does not pay, the patient will be held responsible. If the insurer does not pay within a reasonable period of time, demand payment from the patient, and continue making demands until the debt is satisfied.

Finally, in order to avoid statute of limitations battles, use a conservative approach when calculating the statute of limitations. The earliest point upon which a statute of limitations could begin to run is the date of treatment. The safest course of action, then, is to target your collection efforts so you are prepared to file a lawsuit no later than the limitation period for the cause of action that has the shortest statute of limitations. Thus, if the action you pursue has a statute of limitations of five years, be sure to file a lawsuit well within five years of the date of service, not of the date of initial billing.

Q: Who pays for services after a divorce?

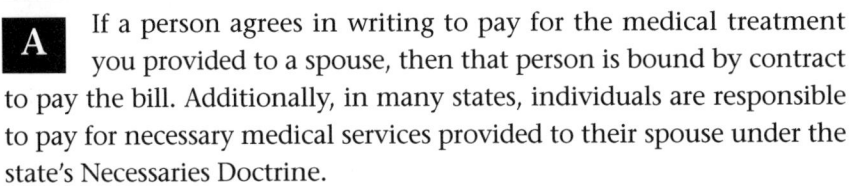

A: If a person agrees in writing to pay for the medical treatment you provided to a spouse, then that person is bound by contract to pay the bill. Additionally, in many states, individuals are responsible to pay for necessary medical services provided to their spouse under the state's Necessaries Doctrine.

Key: The parties must be married at the time services are rendered. There is little case law on the question of whether marital status at the time of the collection efforts has any impact on the responsibility for the debt, and the case law that exists is very old. But according to the old case law, marital status at the time of debt is irrelevant as long as the patient and spouse were legally married at the time the debt was incurred.

In your efforts to hold a spouse responsible for payment under a state's Necessaries Doctrine, you are likely to encounter two defenses:
1. Services were not medically necessary.
2. Charges are excessive.

In your efforts to hold an ex-spouse liable, two additional issues could arise:
1. The divorce decree may specify which spouse must pay the outstanding claim.
2. If there was a delay between the time of services and the time you began collection efforts, and that delay prejudiced the ex-spouse, you could be barred from recovery.

Tip: Send the patient's bill and begin follow-up procedures in a timely manner. If you are aware of a patient going through divorce or child custody proceedings, flag the patient's file as a priority to prevent costly delays.

Q Under what circumstances can a hospital discontinue care for a patient?

A The federal law relevant to this question is the Emergency Medical Treatment and Active Labor Act (EMTALA). This act applies to hospitals that have an emergency department. Under this act, a hospital is required to provide an "appropriate medical screening examination within the capability of the hospital's emergency department, including ancillary services routinely available to the hospital's emergency department," to determine whether an emergency medical condition exists. If an emergency medical condition exists, the hospital is required to provide whatever examination and treatment is necessary to stabilize the patient.

Under this act, a hospital is not liable for not performing tests or treatment it does not have the capability to perform. A hospital is also not obligated to treat a patient if the patient (or patient's representative) refuses to consent to an examination or treatment. In the latter situation, the act requires that the hospital attempt to get the patient's written informed consent to refuse treatment.

If a hospital decides to transfer a patient, the transfer cannot be made until the patient is stabile, except under certain limited exceptions. If a patient asks to be transferred, a hospital can transfer the patient before stabilizing if the hospital informs the patient of the risk of transfer and the patient requests in writing to be transferred. Also, a patient can be transferred before stabilization if a physician certifies that the risks of transfer are outweighed by the benefits that a patient could experience at the receiving facility. In order to transfer under these conditions, the receiving facility must be able to provide some treatment or test that the transferring facility cannot, and that treatment or test must be necessary to minimize the risks to the patient's and/or unborn child's health. The receiving facility must have space and qualified clinicians available to treat, and it must agree to the transfer. All medical records must accompany the patient to the receiving facility. The transfer must be performed by qualified medical personnel, and the necessary life support measures must be available throughout the transport.

Reasoning behind the law: The purpose of EMTALA is to ensure all persons have access to emergency medical treatment, regardless of ability to pay. However, plaintiffs often attempt to use this act as a basis for medical malpractice liability because the act may set a higher standard of care. In medical malpractice, the standard by which the alleged negligent treatment is judged is whether the care fell within the generally accepted standard of practice. If, hypothetically speaking, all doctors discharge indigent patients from the emergency room after giving only a cursory screening and without providing stabilizing care, that is the standard of care and there would be no medical malpractice for the consequences. *However, under EMTALA, regardless of the generally accepted standard of care, a cursory screening of an indigent patient is not sufficient.* An indigent patient must receive the same screening and have access to the same tests and emergency treatment that any patient who comes through your doors would receive, and an indigent patient must be stabilized before he or she can be discharged. Success with using EMTALA in this manner is rare, but it could work given the right set of facts.

After the emergency screening and stabilizing treatment is performed, EMTALA does not mandate that additional treatment be provided. However, some state and local laws require that a hospital provide free treatment to indigent patients and/or provide a certain amount of charity care. Before you can develop any policies relating to discharge or transfer of indigent patients, you should check with your general counsel to determine the full nature of your obligations.

Even if there is no state or local law requiring you to treat indigent patients following stabilization of their medical condition, you may be at risk of civil liability for discharging a patient due to lack of financial resources if the patient requires additional medical treatment. It is difficult to compile a checklist of things to do to avoid liability. However, there are a number of steps that should be taken before discontinuing treatment under such circumstances:

Inform the patient that he or she will be responsible for paying for treatment, and then give the option of making payment arrangements. The risks of discharge and/or discontinuing treatment should be explained in a manner that the patient can understand. If the patient is not capable of understanding those risks, guardianship issues should be considered. Adequate alternate treatment should be arranged if the patient elects to discontinue treatment. If treatment is truly appropriate and the patient elects to discontinue due to financial reasons, an against-medical-advice discharge should be considered. Social services and/or financial counselors should be made available to assist in arranging for financial assistance, such as medical assistance. Obviously, this is not a comprehensive list, and the circumstances of each case will dictate the necessary considerations.

Appendix C

Starting an In-House Bank Loan Program

Nearly 60 percent of the nation's hospitals report using some type of patient financing program for self-pay balances, with about 30 percent of those financing options a bank note or bank financing program.

Still, a significant percentage of self-pay accounts receivable — nearly 27 percent — is routed through no-interest hospital financing programs.[1]

As self-pay becomes an increasingly significant issue for health care providers, due to rising copayment, coinsurance, and deductible amounts or due to insufficient or lack of insurance coverage, the need to effectively manage and collect self-pay balances is of growing concern.

One of the greatest challenges for hospital collections staff is not pure self-pay accounts for the uninsured, who may be candidates for Title XIX or charity. Rather, it is self-pay balances owed by patients who have insurance but who also have large copayment or deductible requirements. Although these patients may be employed and carry insurance coverage, they may not have enough income to make payment in full on their portion of the bill.

Bank financing is an attractive option because it allows patients to pay over time, providers receive immediate payment, and the responsibility for collecting self-pay balances is placed in the hands of a financial institution with experience and clout when it comes to collecting on consumer debt.

Bank financing has been an option for patients at four acute care hospitals (1,400 licensed beds combined) served by a central business office within the Texas Health System. Doug Booth, director of business operations and collections for the four facilities, says the move to bank financing in the early 1990s has played a significant role in improving financial indicators for the four hospitals.

At the close of 1999, four key financial indicators reported by Booth for the four hospitals were better than national averages, except for charity — outcomes that are possible due in no small part to the bank financing option available to patients. The four indicators and the national averages follow:

Financial Indicator	Texas Health System 1999 Year-End Data for Four Acute Care Hospitals	National Average Fourth Quarter 1999 Data
Nets days revenue outstanding	62.4 days	66.9 days
Aging receivables less than 90 days	80 percent	68.1 percent
Percent of gross revenue written off as bad debt	2.7 percent	3.9 percent
Percent of gross revenue written off as charity	3.1 percent	1.5 percent

Source: Data from Texas Health System, Dallas, Texas, and *HARA (Hospital Accounts Receivable Analysis),* fourth quarter 1999, Aspen Publishers, Inc.

Extending a bank financing option to patients creates the classic win-win-win situation. Patients gain from the ability to take advantage of a manageable payment plan. Providers gain from receiving immediate cash flow, which allows the money to work for them immediately. Banks gain from accumulating interest on the accounts, which bolsters their revenue and investment income potential.

More specifically, for patients, the benefits include:

- relieving patients of the anxiety of how debt for medical services will be paid
- creating a payment plan that fits within the patient's budget
- offering a repayment plan at interest rates lower than most credit card rates
- creating a vehicle to incorporate future medical charges into an existing loan

For the bank, the benefits include:
- improved revenues by adding new interest-paying customers as clients
- limiting risk of medical finance accounts as delinquent accounts are sold back to the provider

For providers, bank loan financing benefits include:
- improved cash flow as self-pay balances handled through the bank loan program are paid immediately
- improved investment earnings due to increased cash flow
- reduced overhead costs as the cost of collection of self-pay balances handled through the bank loan program is borne by the bank
- improved patient relations as the provider offers patients a convenient payment option that fits within their budget at interest rates lower than most credit card rates
- reduced patient complaints tied to hospital collection efforts as the bank and not the provider is asking patients for money

FULL-RECOURSE PROGRAM PAYS OFF FOR PROVIDERS EVEN IF BUYBACK REQUIRED

A key benefit for providers and banking institutions alike is that the vast majority of loans are paid as making payments to the bank holds a high priority for consumers who seek to preserve or rebuild a good credit history. The average recourse rate, or percent of loans that default and must be repurchased by providers, runs about 15 percent, according to John Konstantos, vice president of Corus Medical Finance, a health care financing program that operates through Corus Bank.

Even if recourse rates are higher, providers still stand to gain. An account typically remains with the bank for up to 10 months. If a patient defaults on the loan, the provider has had the opportunity to earn interest on that income during that 10-month period, in addition to saving money by not having to dedicate human and material resources to attempt collection on the account. Overall, providers are not any worse off by routing patients through a bank financing program and often are better off even if an account is repurchased.

The Corus Medical Finance Program is one of the oldest in the country and serves more than 120 hospitals in more than 30 states. With nearly two decades of experience, the program has established a proven positive track record in securing payment from patients with self-pay balances and in providing direct financial benefits to providers.

Based on its experience with contracting health care provider institutions, Corus analyzed a bank loan program on a $1 million portfolio vs. in-house handling of that same value of self-pay balances, and calculated that the bank loan program can result in a net difference of more than $400,000 in positive cash flow for a provider. This positive cash flow is realized as far fewer dollars are sent to a collection agency, resulting in a significant reduction in the amount written off as bad debt. Corus's analysis is detailed in the following table:

Corus		In-House	
Contracts	$1,000,000	Receivables	$1,000,000
Recourse	$(200,000)	Uncollected in year 1	$(700,000)
Subtotal	**$800,000**	**Subtotal**	**$300,000**
Sent to collection agency	$200,000	Sent to collection agency	$700,000
Recovery amount	$40,000	Recovery amount	$280,000
Cost of recovery	$(10,000)	Cost of recovery	$(70,000)
Net recovery	$30,000	Net recovery	$210,000
Subtotal	**$830,000**	**Subtotal**	**$510,000**
Recourse costs	$(5,260)	In-house collection costs	$(60,000)

continues

	Corus		In-House
Investment income potential	$48,000	Investment income potential	$18,000
Net cash to provider	$872,740	Net cash to provider	$468,000
Net difference	$404,740		
Written off to bad debt	$160,000	Written off to bad debt	$420,000

Assumptions
• Rate of recourse for Corus Medical Finance Program: 20 percent
• Self-pay funds uncollectible for in-house program: 70 percent
• In-house collections cost: $0.20 per dollar collected (Source: *HARA [Hospital Accounts Receivable Analysis]*, first quarter 1999, Aspen Publishers, Inc.)
• Cost to outsource to collection agency: $0.25 per dollar collected
• Recovery rate for outside collection agency: 20 percent for Corus, 40 percent for hospital
• Recourse cost: prime rate for 120 days
• Rate of return on funds available for investment: 6 percent (not assumed for collections)

This analysis assumes an existing $1 million portfolio of Corus contracts vs. the same amount of accounts receivable managed in-house. The $700,000 not collected does not reflect bad debt, but rather the amount not paid by patients in the first year. This analysis helps to establish a framework to assess the value of a bank loan program, with assumptions based on the Corus Medical Finance Program's experience with other hospitals, and may not reflect a specific facility's results.

Courtesy of Corus Medical Finance, Chicago, Illinois. |

Another method to calculate the benefits of a bank loan program is to analyze what it costs a provider to carry a self-pay balance over time.

Consider that a $5,000 balance paid at $50 a month will take a little over eight years to be paid in full. However, during that time, provider losses incurred to manage that account in-house mount significantly when inflation and lost investment earnings are considered. A $5,000 balance paid over eight years will net a provider only slightly more than half that amount once money lost to inflation, lost interest, and costs to bill are factored into the equation. The cost of carrying various balances long term is shown in the table on the following page.

Given the improved net cash disbursement to providers by sending self-pay balances through a bank financing program, it becomes apparent that it is in a health care delivery organization's best financial interest to pursue this receivables management option and maximize participation in such a program. Profitability improves as collection expenses and bad debt decline and cash flow increases.

IDENTIFYING A QUALIFIED BANKING PARTNER

To secure the benefits of bank financing as a tool for effective accounts receivable management and collections, providers must identify a qualified banking partner. Key elements to seek in a bank financing partner is a track record in medical finance programs and a commitment to grow with the hospital's needs in this area.

In addition, a bank financing partner must have a significant volume of medical finance contracts for it to be profitable while extending lower interest rates and keeping other related fees low. Lacking volume, a bank may require higher set-up and training fees to the provider, as well as a higher front-end discount for contracts received. For instance, with a $1,000 contract at a 5 percent discount rate, the provider receives $950 from the bank. This discount may be higher if the bank financing partner lacks sufficient volume, thus cutting into the amount disbursed to the provider.

Typically, front-end discounts cost providers from 3 percent to 8 percent of the total loan amount with a bank. This discount, however, is offset by injecting immediate cash flow to the provider, as well as by eliminating costs for the provider to service and collect on the account.

The bank partner likely will require up to three years of audited fi-

Cost To Carry Patient Balances Long Term

Patient Balance	Monthly Payment	No. of Monthly Payments	Money Lost to Inflation	Low Interest	Cost To Bill	Total Cost To Carry Account Long Term	Actual Net Payment to Provider
$150	$10	15	$11	$7	$8	$26	$124
$620	$20	31	$50	$75	$25	$151	$469
$1,500	$35	43	$151	$226	$34	$411	$1,089
$5,000	$50	100	$915	$1,373	$71	$2,360	$2,640
$10,000	$25	400	$6,815	$10,223	$281	$17,320	$7,320
$15,000	$100	150	$3,889	$5,834	$105	$9,828	$5,172

Source: *How To Set Up an Effective Bank Loan Program*, Aspen Publishers, Inc., © 1994.

nancial statements. This data is used to determine whether the health care delivery organization meets the bank's criteria in extending credit.

The bank will charge providers set-up and training fees, which can range from $250 to $750. In addition, the medical finance partner will provide program materials, including:
- credit application forms
- loan contract forms
- procedure manuals to be used by financial counselors, collections, registration employees, and other employees charged with implementing the program
- brochures and other materials to educate patients about the medical finance program and its benefits
- monthly reports of new loans and outstanding loans with aged balances, and quarterly recaps of new loan totals

REVISING PAYMENT AND COLLECTIONS POLICY

Perhaps the most critical step in setting up a bank financing program involves in-house planning for the conversion from carrying self-pay accounts at no interest to setting up a bank loan with an affixed interest rate for patients.

Moving away from carrying no-interest, self-pay balances long term requires a commitment by the institution at all levels. If patients are accustomed to paying the hospital a small amount each month at no interest, resources must be dedicated to educating patients about new policies that require payment in full or within a tight payment window. Patients unable to pay within those parameters then can opt for bank financing.

A full commitment to bank financing is a must or the full benefits of a bank financing program will not be realized. This commitment must permeate the organization, with endorsements from top executives and buy-in from front-line employees who must implement the policy and ensure the bank financing program is used to its greatest potential.

Collection and payment policies must be reviewed and revised to incorporate bank financing and to make it a priority as a desirable option for patients who cannot afford to pay in full at the time of service.

Within the Texas Health System, payment policies that incorporated bank financing were crafted not only to improve the bottom line, but also to ensure that patient-pay financial obligations were communicated with patients early in the process. This conveys the idea to patients that the provider expects to be paid and will work with patients to that end.

Booth reports that the options for patients at the four hospitals under his purview are simple and clear. Patients may:
- pay in full with a credit card, check, cash, or money order
- pay in four equal payments over three months
- set up a bank loan to pay high-dollar self-pay balances over several months or several years

If the latter option is chosen, the patient is able to establish an easy repayment plan that fits within his or her budget. Employees enter into the system the length of the bank loan term to identify monthly payment amounts. Or, if patients indicate an amount they can afford to pay each month, that amount is entered to calculate the term of the bank loan. With the bank loan term and monthly payments determined and accepted by the patient, the provider is able to refer to the bank a loan candidate poised and able to make payments. Meanwhile, the hospital system receives the cash amount of the loan, minus a discount, immediately from the bank.

EMPLOYEE EDUCATION AND TRAINING ARE CRITICAL FOR SUCCESS OF BANK FINANCING PROGRAM

Educating employees on the reason for offering a bank financing option and its benefits to all involved parties is also critical. Employees must understand and embrace bank financing as a collections tool in order to sell it effectively to patients. This education must include specific training on how to discuss the bank loan option with patients.

For instance, how the issue is broached with patients can make the difference between whether patients choose the bank loan option or decline, saying they will attempt to pay on their own, a choice that could leave the provider with an aging receivable that may ultimately turn into bad debt.

It's all in a turn of a phrase, according to Booth. Employees are trained to be positive and promote the bank loan program. For instance, employees don't calculate the patient balance and then say, "Do you need a loan to cover this?" Such a question immediately puts patients on the defensive.

Rather, employees identify the patient's financial obligations and review the various options for payment. Among the options presented is the hospital's medical finance or medical assistance program, and it is communicated to patients as a positive option that allows them to pay their balances over time at interest rates lower than most credit card rates.

The banking partner often extends employee training when setting up a medical financing program with a provider, and builds the cost into the set-up fee.

Hospital employees are given the means to illustrate for patients the payment schedule and cost to finance the self-pay balance. This is important information to share with patients to allow them to make an educated decision in choosing a payment plan. See sample payment scenarios in the table on the following page.

BANK FINANCING BASICS

Once a banking partner is identified and employees are educated and trained, implementing a bank financing program is fairly straightforward. Here's how it works:

- ***Patients with self-pay balances are screened*** by hospital staff to determine if they are indeed candidates for the medical financing program. The level of screening that takes place within the hospital can vary. It is important to determine through the credit application process the patient's willingness and ability to pay. In general, if patients agree to the bank loan program and have a steady source of income, they are candidates for the program.
- Hospital employees **work with patients to determine monthly payment amounts.** The monthly amount or the length of time required to pay the debt can be determined by how much pa-

Loan Payment Plans

Patient Balance	12 Months Monthly payment	12 Months Total paid	18 Months Monthly payment	18 Months Total paid	24 Months Monthly payment	24 Months Total paid	36 Months Monthly payment	36 Months Total paid	48 Months Monthly payment	48 Months Total paid
$1,000	$90	$1,080	$62	$1,119	n/a	n/a	n/a	n/a	n/a	n/a
$1,500	$135	$1,621	$93	$1,678	$72	$1,737	$52	$1,859	n/a	n/a
$2,000	$180	$2,161	$124	$2,237	$97	$2,316	$69	$2,479	$55	$2,648
$3,000	$270	$3,241	$186	$3,356	$145	$3,474	$103	$3,718	$83	$3,972
$5,000	$450	$5,401	$311	$5,594	$241	$5,790	$172	$6,196	$138	$6,619

Source: Data from *How To Set Up an Effective Bank Loan Program*, Aspen Publishers, Inc., © 1994.

tients state they are able to pay each month or by the length of time over which they wish to pay the loan.
- ***Bank loan applications*** with the desired monthly payment amounts are ***submitted electronically to the bank***. The bank is under contract to accept all applications as medical finance contracts. Medical finance programs are typically full-recourse programs and thus pose minimal risk for the bank.
- ***Provider reimbursement*** is made electronically through direct deposit, typically within a day or less. Payment is the loan amount minus a front-end discount.
- ***Patients receive a coupon book in the mail*** from the bank, with an introduction to the program and the payment plan established for the patient. The bank may secure payment terms to set up the account as a direct debit from the patient's savings or checking account, if preferred by the patient.

Corus has two medical finance programs. One is for a standard minimum loan amount of $400, with a minimum monthly payment of $35. Under the small-dollar program, the minimum loan amount is $200, with a minimum monthly payment of $25. An additional front-end discount of 2 percent applies to small-dollar accounts because of the shortened loan term, which reduces the amount of interest collected.

Ideally, patients should be identified as bank loan candidates prior to or at the time of service by registration employees. Depending on the structure of the provider organization, registration employees may initiate a bank loan agreement with a patient. Or registration employees may identify bank loan candidates, referring patients to a financial counselor to set up the payment plan.

However, there are always exceptions. Emergency department patients and direct admits, for example, who will have significant patient-pay balances may be directed toward a bank loan program during the patient stay, upon discharge, or after discharge during the follow-up collections process.

CREDIT APPLICATION ELEMENTS

Key data to gather during the credit and loan application process is information required to collect on the account. This includes complete patient demographic data and employment information, as well as coapplicant information as appropriate. The goal is to evaluate an applicant's ability to pay, and thus the potential for successful collections through the bank loan program.

While credit screening processes will vary by hospital — some intensely scrutinize bank loan candidates while others perform a very limited screening process — it is critical that the process includes gathering the essential information the bank partner will need to establish and collect an account.

A sample patient credit application follows (an abbreviated form may be used as long as essential demographic and employment data are gathered):

Sample Patient Credit Application

Date: _____
Total loan amount: _____
No. of months: _____
Monthly payment amount: _____

PATIENT INFORMATION
Name: _____
Birth date: _____ SS#: _____ Dependents: _____
Address: _____
City: _____ State: _____ Zip: _____
Telephone: _____
Mortgage holder/landlord name:
_____
Address: _____ Telephone: _____
How long at current address? _____
Previous address: _____
How long at previous address? _____

continues

EMPLOYMENT INFORMATION
Employer:_____
Address:_____
City: _____ State: _____ Zip: _____
Telephone: _____
Current position: _____ Years with employer: _____
Supervisor's name and title:_____
Present annual salary: _____ Other income: _____
Previous employer:_____
Address: _____ Telephone: _____

FINANCIAL AND CREDIT INFORMATION
Checking account #: _____ Financial institution: _____
Address:_____
City: _____ State: _____ Zip: _____
Savings account #: _____ Financial institution: _____
Address: _____

CURRENT MONTHLY PAYMENT OBLIGATIONS
Please list all outstanding debts, e.g., auto loans, credit card accounts, etc.

Total amount owed	Present balance	Monthly payment	Amount past due
1. _____	_____	_____	_____
2. _____	_____	_____	_____
3. _____	_____	_____	_____
4. _____	_____	_____	_____
5. _____	_____	_____	_____
6. _____	_____	_____	_____

Have you ever filed for bankruptcy or Chapter 13? _____ If yes, please explain: _____
Do you have any judgment filed against you? _____ If yes, please explain: _____

continues

> CO-APPLICANT INFORMATION
> Name:_____
> Birth date: _____ SS#: _____ Dependents: _____
> Address:_____
> City: _____ State: _____ Zip: _____
> Telephone: _____
>
> Applicant signature: _____
> Co-applicant signature: _____
> Date: _____
>
> Source: *How To Set Up an Effective Bank Loan Program*, Aspen Publishers, Inc., © 1994.

With a credit application in hand, provider employees can take some extra steps to evaluate the application to determine the patient's ability to pay, as well as the potential that the patient may be a collection risk. These additional three steps are as follows:

1. **Verify information provided on the application.** Start with the basics — the home telephone number and address. They can be verified through the telephone directory and/or a reverse directory for the area. If either the address or the telephone number is incorrect, there is a good chance other information on the application, or its entirety, is fraudulent.

    Also verify the applicant's work telephone number and determine if the applicant is a current employee. If the applicant is not currently employed, determine if that is a permanent or temporary situation.

2. **Compare income to total expenses listed.** This step helps identify whether the patient has the financial ability to incorporate additional debt with existing debt obligations.

3. **Seek a co-applicant if there is any doubt** the applicant may be unable to fulfill the terms of the loan.

Some other factors to consider in evaluating collection risk include:

- **frequent change of address**
  On the flip and positive side is home ownership. This indicates stability and a greater chance the debt will be collected. However, it is important to review the size of the mortgage in weighing collection risk.
- **frequent change of jobs**
  Typically, three years on a job indicates occupational stability.
- **earnings**
- **marital status**
  This can be a positive indicator as marriage connotes a willingness to assume responsibility, although it is no guarantee. Still, married people tend to be better collection risks.
- **age**
  Debtors under age 25 pose the greatest collection risk. Financial responsibility tends to improve with age. A patient must be 18 to obtain a bank loan, unless someone is willing to co-sign the loan.
- **financial history**
  The patient's past track record in repaying outstanding debts is a key indicator of his or her willingness and ability to take responsibility for repaying a bank loan. This information may be available within your own records if the patient has been treated at the facility before. In addition, a credit check and banking references can shed light on prior financial behavior. Keep in mind, however, that a patient's future potential to pay is more important than past history.

THE PATIENT DIALOGUE

As noted earlier, how the issue of medical financing is broached with patients can determine whether patients will indeed choose a bank loan payment option. The following sample dialogue illustrates how to keep the conversation positive, and thus increase the likelihood patients will choose the bank loan option:

Financial counselor: The self-pay portion of your medical bill will be $1,500 and is due in full upon discharge. We have several payment options. You may pay in full with cash, check, credit card, or money order. Or you may defer payment over time through our medical finance program with Alexander Bank. This program allows you to make monthly payments over time to fit your budget.

Patient: I would prefer to pay you directly, to avoid interest charges.

Financial counselor: I understand. However, our facility is unable to finance patient balances, which is why we have contracted with Alexander Bank, which offers interest rates below most credit card rates. Many patients choose this option, as payments can be tailored to fit your budget. The interest rate is only 14.5 percent, compared to up to 21 percent charged by many credit card companies.

Patient: But how much will I actually be paying in interest if I use a bank loan?

Financial counselor: That depends on the term of the loan. If you pay the $1,500 within a year, the interest cost would only be about $120.

Patient: Still, that's a lot of money. Maybe I should speak with my own banker.

Financial counselor: You certainly may. But keep in mind, this would be an unsecured loan, unlike a car loan. Many banks shy away from unsecured loans.

Patient: I see. What do I have to do to use your program? Do I have to go to the bank myself?

Financial counselor: No, I can take care of everything right here. You simply need to complete this credit application. Then, once we determine the amount you would like to pay each month, I'll fax the contract to the bank and it will be set in motion. You will receive a payment coupon book from the bank in a couple of weeks, and you're set. Plus, should you or someone in your family need future medical services at our facility, any new charges can be incorporated into the existing loan.

Patient: OK. But my credit record isn't great.

Financial counselor: As long as you are willing and able to make payments on this loan, that shouldn't be a problem. And, in fact, this will work to your benefit as it is an easy way to rebuild a good credit rating. Just make sure you make your payments on time and you will build a good credit history.

Of course, actual conversations with patients may not go as smoothly as in the sample because emotions and anxiety tend to run high when medical treatment is required and unexpected health care expenses threaten a patient's financial well-being.

The key is to always remain positive and remind patients that the medical financing option allows them to remain in control of their finances because the payment plan is crafted to fit within their budget.

BANK AND HOSPITAL COLLECTION POLICIES IN SYNC

Although a bank financing puts the responsibility for collecting from patients in the hands of the bank, the loan has roots with the provider. Patients will remember that, and so should the provider. A bank loan is not an opportunity to wash your hands of a debt. Rather, it is an effective receivables management tool and should be viewed and embraced as such. With this in mind, providers should ensure the bank's collection policies jibe with that of the health care delivery organization.

Collection policies under bank loan programs typically allow for a five-day and ten-day past-due reminder notice if payment is not received on time. At 20 days, collection letters are mailed and telephone calls to patients are initiated.

Still, the bank needs to be open to being flexible in its collection practices for health care accounts. Inasmuch as providers want a bank to act like a bank, which aids collection success in medical finance programs, Konstantos notes the banking partner still must be sensitive to the fact that these loans are for health care obligations and that extenuating circumstances may exist.

CONCLUSION

For a bank financing program to be effective, provider organizations must commit to using it as a vehicle to manage and collect on patient-pay balances. Patients who cannot pay in full within 30 days should be referred to the bank loan program. This message must be consistent and firm, or patients will recognize that they can still skirt the issue of payment by dragging out repayment plans long term.

The benefits are many, to all involved parties. Patients, providers, and the bank stand to gain. Providers perhaps garner the greatest benefits as bank financing allows them to extend to patients an attractive payment option for outstanding balances that loom large and overwhelming. This patient relations coup then reflects in the bottom line, as cash flow improves, bad debt is reduced, and collection costs decline.

REFERENCE

1. *HARA (Hospital Accounts Receivable Analysis)*, third quarter 1999 (Gaithersburg, MD: Aspen Publishers, Inc.).

SOURCES CONSULTED

Doug Booth, director of business operations and collections, Texas Health System, Dallas, Texas.

John Konstantos, vice president, Corus Medical Finance, Chicago, Illinois.